# The Telling Stones

# The
# Telling
# Stones

*including* **The Mad Bastard's Guide to Enlightenment**

**Riktam Barry**

NON-DUALITY PRESS
UNITED KINGDOM

THE TELLING STONES

First edition published March 2011 by NON-DUALITY PRESS

Cover photograph by John Gitsham

NON-DUALITY PRESS | PO Box 2228 | Salisbury | SP2 2GZ
United Kingdom

ISBN: 978-0-9566432-5-4

www.non-dualitypress.com

## With Gratitude

To thank a few of many, first the inspiring word-dancers, Douglas Adams, Leonard Cohen, Russell Hoban, Richard Brautigan and PG Wodehouse.

Steven Richardson for the seed that started it, and Alex Petkov who, years later, read the very dusty manuscript and hassled me till I sent it here.

John Gitsham for taking the cover photograph.

# Contents

## THE MAD BASTARD'S GUIDE TO ENLIGHTENMENT

# MAX GOES TO WOODSTOCK

*I'm always a bit sad to have missed the moments that have become the centres of hippie memory, but although the wave broke a little later in Australia we didn't really miss anything relevant. The entire impetus for the rejection of the straight world's bathwater and babies was the same media input in the whole of the western world.*

*I* love to visit Max. His house is perfect. A stone cottage with small windows, not too tidy outside with its random wood-heap and falling tin shed, but stepping inside is like getting out of a time machine set for the mid-Sixties. There are pretty little found objects catching the light on the windowsill, sari curtains, wooden surfaces everywhere, all the colour of honey. The chairs are square wooden affairs, each painted a different pastel colour. Sometimes a plain tablecloth, but mostly, like today, a clean wooden table top.

There is always a pot of tea to be had. So we have one.

There is an unstated conversational convention here that keeps a stream of consciousness going forever. Max simply starts talking wherever he left off last time.

"I nearly went to Woodstock," he says, in a slow, mellow voice, a considering-things-in-the-background sort of sound to it.

Last time I visited him, there was a friend with us who was living near Woodstock at the time but didn't bother going. He had told stories of his neighbour who had arrived there several days early and camped for the duration in her

1

Volkswagen Kombi. She had been hassled from day two by people begging for water, and robbed of most of the van's removable contents when she stayed away overnight – nearer the stage.

The whole thing sounded awful, but according to him she just loved it. "Wouldn't have missed so much positive one-purpose collective consciousness for anything."

The young of the Sixties were cursed with the huge contradiction between the world events of the day as depicted on their brand new graphic television, and the values insisted on by their parents. It was all a bit much for some, and from the rejection of straight world, its madness and constraints grew the field of vast possibility.

I never feel confident that Max is telling the truth, but it's always a good story so I don't insult him by wondering this aloud.

"I was in Afghanistan about three months before, camped near the mountains, waiting for a bloke to meet me for a little business."

"Ah, business, Max," I reply in that special affirmative, get-on-with-it voice.

"I wasn't buying dope, mate; I had a few rifles to sell, early Kalashnikovs. This American bloke I was with had bought them at a market, with my money mind you, that sort of committed me to helping him sell them."

Jesus, Max is a gunrunner! He just looks like an old hippie.

"We had a lot of faith then, man. What we did was wander into the mountains looking for some bugger to buy these guns. We ran out of food in a couple of days. The Yank said he was going to a music festival after the money came. Woodstock in New York State, via Kabul and London. I was a bit interested so I decided to go with him. He left sometime that night, must have walked. I still had both the camels in the morning. The guns too."

Max is telling this story in a monotone, slow and careful. No dramatic intonation, no emotion, only a little grin and nod between sentences. This is why I can believe him. He fits my idea of an old Australian storyteller. No campfire, no bush; it all happens in little kitchens with tea and a smoke. The cat comes in, sits on my lap and starts to purr. I pat. We have more tea.

"When I woke up, there was another camp about two hundred yards away, a lot of people, noise and camels, even a fire. I was a bit worried; I thought they might have killed the Yank when he went for a piss. I sat there wondering what to do with these rifles and no food when this fantastic smell of fresh coffee hit. I was going to introduce myself to next door when someone came up, no English, pointing at me and at the empty cup he was carrying. I reckon they took pity on me huddled in a blanket. So I went over."

I have to take a leak. Tea. Everywhere you go in this time warp there is tea. I reckon the strongest bladders in the world must belong to hippies. Max, for instance, never goes. Maybe he's got a bag. I'll ask. I'm not having another smoke, that's for sure.

The toilet is perfect too. White paint on walls of stone, textured with dust. The cistern is attached high on the wall with a chain. On the end of the chain, the large knob from a brass bed. I flush.

Arriving back in the kitchen I am overwhelmed by the need to explain to Max how I am seeing his house and where it fits in my personal anthropology. I sit down.

"Always good to see you, man," I say. Max looks up from rolling another joint.

"Yeah, you too."

We smoke again, the cat settles on me once more, and starts to gently push its claws in and out of my leg. Max is talking again. I look up and see that he has made more tea.

"There was only four of them, but they were happy, loud, Middle Eastern brothers, you know. The oldest one, Sam, spoke English better than me. He asked how come I was there. I told him I was on my way to Woodstock. When they found out it was a music festival, they got excited and started bringing all sorts of weird instruments out of cloth bags. We all had a smoke from the biggest block of hash I had ever seen, then played and sang most of the day. Shit, that was killer smoke."

Max lights the joint again, takes a Rastafarian size toke and passes it to me. I smoke and he goes on.

"We stayed there the night. Next day I spoke to Sam about the guns. He knew a guy in the mountains. I didn't want to go, so two of his brothers left us, grinning and promising lots of dollars. I knew I wouldn't get dollars, only westerners pay in dollars. Sam, me and Mustafa...."

I laugh.

"No, dead set! That was the bugger's name – nice bloke, too. We all went to Kabul to wait for the brothers... fuck you; I'm not telling you their names."

I look up to see Max is grinning. I was worried – thought I had rattled him. Not so.

"Sam's house was great. I could never have found it without him. Way down in that end of town that you'd be too scared to go to if you weren't local. I got fed, we smoked a lot of very fine local hash and somebody bought my camels. I was very happy. I had money even if the nameless brothers didn't front."

I give Max the last of the joint and he grabs a leather thong hanging around his neck and pulls a roach clip up from under his shirt. I haven't seen anything like it for years. This one is a beauty, a little slip collar; it all looks like silver. In one seamless movement Max pops the end of the joint into it, reduces it to nothing with one breath, flicks the roach into the ashtray and drops the clip straight down his shirt again. I feel like an archaeologist.

"They did, of course. Hardly anyone ripped you off then. It was before."

I was puzzled.

"Before what, man?"

"Shit, before everything. There weren't any tourists at the edges of the world then, all the cultures were still different and just interested in each other. The biggest thing was there was hardly anyone anywhere. I reckon the thing that we missed that did us and all our dreams in proper, was that nobody knew how crowded the planet was going to get. That's why I live out here. This is a great country. Not many people, nobody shoots at you, and much as it would like to, the government is still not throwing people into jail for disagreeing with it. All this because since the Sixties, the population of the world has more than doubled. The resources are the same, so a nice life is harder to get with all the extra people crawling about."

Max gets up and goes to the tall cupboard. This is as passionate as I've ever heard him; he isn't sad, but clear that the place that he knew is no longer there.

"There's less stuff for everyone now and they are getting meaner all the time."

He takes a bottle of red wine down from a shelf. I am definitely here for the night.

"Anyway, it wasn't like this before. I made a fair bit of money on the guns and decided to get some more and sell them on. No need to hurry, the woman up the road kept bringing me food, we got to be lovers, and all of us were one big happy family. Woodstock was still nearly three months away, I had an upstairs room with a view over the Market Square, and there was always a nice breeze. Rabhia and me were having a ball and there was more hash than I had ever seen. I didn't have to do anything; I just paid a little rent."

We are drinking now. I hate to mix my intoxicants, it gets confusing. Max, however, is without any such puritanical viewpoint.

"I learned to speak a fair amount of Pashto during the next weeks. Me and Sam went on a gun run. We used his camels so he took extra money, and we all smoked Afghani hash after dinner every night."

I can see where this is going. Max pours more wine for us both. He drinks almost the whole glass, swallows, and says with deep conviction, "Where else in the world can you get wine this good for ten bucks? Nowhere, man."

It *is* good. I want to know why he left Afghanistan. I have known Max for thirty years and during the early part there was no real trouble there. I ask him.

"That was really sad, man. Apparently when Sam and I went to the arms market we were seriously imposing on someone else's business territory. Once, okay, but we lifted the quantity to a proper profit-taking number on that second trip. The bloke who had the franchise was looking for us. Sam called a house meeting. I decided to leave the country and after I was gone Sam would tell the proper criminals about the westerner who didn't know any better."

He stands up and takes off to the toilet. I pat the cat and listen to the crickets outside. This is good. I am stoned, at ease and have a little wine in me. I hear Max flush the toilet and sit upright with a start. He comes in and sits down with a sigh.

"She wanted to come, but was too scared to leave Kabul. She was such a beautiful woman. I still wonder if I couldn't have just taken a beating and stayed."

Max has tears. Not proper, but his eyes are wet. I say, "Oh man, I'm sorry."

He smiles. "Shit, man. Who hasn't got a lost great love?"

It's properly dark now, so we finish the wine and cook. Pasta – thank God it isn't fried brown rice. After we eat, we have another joint and sit on the old lounge chairs with tea.

"So where did you go?" I ask.

"London, on my way to Woodstock. I ran into the American guy at the airport. He'd changed his mind in the name of not supporting any nasty capitalist enterprises. He'd also started shooting up since I last saw him."

Max turns and looks directly at me. "Do you know any junkies from then, still alive?"

I have to say that I don't. Lots of old friends come to mind, all gone.

"He's probably dead too," says Max.

Shit, I think. This is a real hidden tragedy; all the junkies I ever met were sharp – they had to be or they went to jail fast. They were intelligent people who might have added something of real value to the culture. Like war dead, just names – but real and talented in memory.

I am feeling a bit maudlin when Max puts another joint in my hand and says, "Come on, man, they couldn't stay, or they would have."

"How come you didn't get to Woodstock then?"

I feel a very strong need to know and hope for a short answer.

"I still had some of the hash from Kabul. I thought I had better have just a bit to relax before I got on the flight to New York. So I spotted it on the end of a fag in the dunny at Heathrow, came out and sat down until the next day. Missed the plane altogether."

"Yeah, that can happen," I say.

Max nods slowly.

"I took it as a sign."

7

## PRINCESS BARBIE AND THE RAJAH

*As a generation we were the least prepared for aging ever. As time passes all kinds of catharsis and traumatic behaviour is being seen as our generation desperately jumps toward anything we see as helping us through this very dark night.*

We are going to India again. My old mate Ross and me, belatedly off to do the guru experience. Belatedly, because it's 1992 and we are going through Bombay to Poona and Rajneesh Ashram. We are at Ross's house, in the kitchen, doing one of my favourite bonding rituals. On the way here I have purchased a six-pack of jam-filled Lamingtons coconut cakes and a tub of cream to drown them in. We are now eating three each from a plate, with garage sale cocktail forks. A cup of tea will follow. The phone rings. Ross gets up and answers.

"Yo." Much listening happens. He then gives our departure details, and says, "Yeah, all right. See you." He hangs up the phone and says to me, grinning like a Cheshire cat, "You're gonna love this, Gimpy."

We have called each other Gimpy for some years now, a sort of abuse affection thing. I know him to have an evil sense of humour, so am now worried about this happiness.

"What?"

"That was Kamala. She's going to catch our flight." I do not believe him. I don't hate this woman; I am, in fact, always glad to see her. After about an hour in her company, however, we are always tense. That isn't why I don't believe him.

"She just got back a week ago, you lying old bastard."

"No, dead set! She is booking her flight today and will get on with us if she can." He knows I'm not easy with Kamala and is enjoying this immensely.

"She's in love with some rich Indian cherry, can't stay away and is keeping us company on her way back to India."

"If she can," I reply. I hope not. Kamala is in no way horrible, but she pushes my buttons because she's a control freak. She has worked for many years selling her sexual favours to the top end of the market and has a perception of men as needy buggers who, because they all want to be in bed with her, are able to be adjusted to suit her current needs. This is never reassessed but laid over every man she knows, including the likes of Ross and me. He doesn't care. In fact, he doesn't seem to mind anything, but after a while with Kamala, I feel as resentful as hell about not being individually recognised. So I hope the plane is full, and say so.

"Gimpy, don't be a weak prick! She's alright."

"No mate, I cannot handle her. I always want to throttle her after about ten minutes."

"Wimp! I'm going to piss myself watching you squirm all the way to India."

He will, too. No mercy or quarter will be given. I can't think how to avoid it so feign surliness and say, "Make the tea."

Ross retires to the kettle and tea tools. I eat Lamingtons. My relationship with him is odd. I have very little in common with him, but our backgrounds are sort of the same. Mine a small country town, now a fairly trendy place to be; and his, a city port also devoured by social change. In India, we travel together well, as the locals somehow sense a common set of values we hold with them. We all know how to behave in a village.

Our adolescences were totally different. Him a real biker, drugs used to get bent, travelled around with a group; and to this day he idly points out bar windows in passing that he has been thrown through. Me a proper hippie, drugs to expand and explore consciousness, much more the social isolate – I didn't even *go* to the bars, let alone come out through the window.

He delivers the tea. "Is that alright old fellow? Is the nasty Kamala pushing your buttons?" I spit coconut on the floor. Peggy, his British Bulldog, snorts across, licks it clean, then looks to me – wanting more. None comes. She retires to the corner and waits. I say nothing and drink tea. Ross is almost paralysed with laughter now.

"Stop it, you bastard, you'll break something."

Ross's body is almost stuffed from bike accidents. That's how I met him. I lived with a good masseuse who was the only person who could stop his back pains. He came and went for months, then one day stayed back for a cup of tea. He was of the group I was estranged from in my youth, not accepted by them in any way, so I was pleased to be welcomed by him. For his part, if asked he would say, "Because you're insane, you bastard."

I reckon the bottom line is the recognition that our time-line-sharing worlds are both dead and so we remind each other of who we are.

He stops laughing and sits up. "This is great. I can't wait!"

Weeks later we are in the departure lounge. I go to the duty free to buy the large bottle of Southern Comfort I will drink in the burning ghats of India. I am very pleased. Kamala has not fronted and we are well past the requested time for arrival. New and spare batteries for everything and I go back out to sit.

Ross has shifted in my absence to another part of the lounge to sit with Kamala, who has arrived in the meantime. He waves. I get our cabin baggage and go to sit with them.

Kamala has already organised the collective trip to Poona

from Bombay airport. She has an Indian friend with a taxi who is meeting us at the airport on arrival.

Kamala is pretty. Blonde wavy hair, nice brown eyes, cute. T-shirt. There are little crows feet starting at the edge of her eyes. Ross looks old; me too. That's what this is about for all of us, some sort of internal self-definition to link the young and the old within and hopefully give sense to whatever comes next.

I have a room booked in Bombay for the first night. The plane arrives at 2.00am so I have no interest in travelling again until late the following morning. I tell her this.

"You'll be excited. It won't be any trouble to go straight through in a taxi, and you can sleep on the way if you need to," Kamala says.

I am already in trouble, my statement ignored. I therefore assume myself unrecognised, and I find it very hard to stand up and insist on my own reality as valid. Kamala is the excited one and will take it as a personal insult that I don't think what she wants is okay for me and we will have a fight. So I say nothing.

Not a good start. I am on holiday, I don't want to fight, and my stomach ties itself in the knot that I recognise as having surrendered my power. Shit!

Ross asks about the Indian lover and Kamala tells us how much she misses him, what good fun they had and how wealthy he is. His surname is the same as the Indian Prime Minister and he has just secured the Nike supply rights to the whole of India. That sounds like proper money to me.

I wander internally until we are on the plane. Kamala has been seated somewhere else due to her late arrival.

"You having fun, mate?" Ross is next to me, grinning again, apparently truly concerned about my levity content.

"Yeah, I'm all right now; thank you very much for asking, bastard."

He makes a few remarks about what a fine time we will all have in Bombay, and I remind him we are now not staying there overnight because there will be a taxi waiting to take us on to Poona.

"In India at two am, how likely is that to happen?" I feel better. It is impossible to organise a late night taxi in India even when the driver is standing in front of you.

"Ah, not at all likely, mate. Thank you. I am much happier now. "

At Singapore duty-free I buy a pair of prismatic binoculars, PDA and a mini-torch with the brightest light I have ever seen. The twentieth century's gadgets are a dream come true; every potential need can be catered for.

Back into the plane and to Bombay Airport, absolutely ready for the knacker's yard and thinking of impending taxis as an event to be avoided at all costs. The torture of customs ("Do you have any gold, sir?") is lessened since last time, as there is now a separate gate for foreigners. To the money booth to change a hundred U.S. dollars into rupees.

As I join the queue, Kamala is peeved because of the delay and wants me to use the black market later. I don't want to do this, as here I will get a certificate of exchange from the Indian Government, which is needed to stay at hotels; the black market just gives you money. She becomes angry and goes to the door leading out, then motions Ross to come with her. He seems not to notice and doesn't move.

"She's in love, mate, very panicky about getting back to Poona to the boyfriend."

"You have to do this here so that you get the exchange certificate, otherwise the hotel won't take your money. Go tell her to chill out, we'll get to bloody Poona." I am strong about what I want if the opposition is absent.

The money comes and I go outside into real India. The humidity and heat as the airport air conditioning is left wraps me up like a blanket. Ah yes, and the smell; I love this place.

Kamala is trying to rid herself of all the street sellers and bag carriers desperate to help and be paid. They thin out quite a bit when Ross and I turn up. We are both big and a bit rough looking from jetlag. Kamala's taxi friend has failed to front and we are now free to go and sleep at my hotel. Good! Kamala is not happy, but is with us.

As we are leaving, a well-dressed young man comes toward us, smiling as though we are his oldest friends, and greets us with the traditional Indian two-handed prayer position salute. I am a sucker for this, because of the implied respect. Its called a Namaste. The literal meaning is "I honour the light within you".

How can anyone who greets people like that have anything but the finest intentions? I make the mistake of looking him in the eye. He nods his head sideways, and with a voice of purest silk, asks, "Is there anything I can help you with, sir? A room? A taxi? Money changing? Smoke, perhaps?"

I am about to say no, thank him and go. Anything organised at the airport gate is a bit suss. Kamala, however, moves in front of me and asks for a Poona taxi. I step away, still committed to my hotel. I would like it if Kamala catches a cab to Poona. They are a recognised service and as reliable as anything is here – a good idea I think. She goes and sees her lover sooner; and I sleep and travel tomorrow.

While I chat to Ross, it comes to light that this man's brother has a little van and will take our entire luggage and us to Poona for only 8,000 Rupees. This is clearly an ambitious claim as the taxi is only 4,000 r/-. I see my sleep vanish and instead of telling her I am not interested, foolishly begin price negotiations with him, demand details of the van, the route and the brother. At the end of several entertaining minutes we are going in a Suzuki van, "Like that one over there, sir".

A little van is pointed at. Not so old, not too bad. The price is down to 2,500 rupees and the driver will not be receiving extra payment from us.

A phone call is made from Airport Security office and thirty-five minutes later a van comes. It is a ruined version of the one used as a sample. A sleepy younger man emerges, and lengthy instructions are given to him in Hindi by his brother, who then returns and says to us, "My brother will take you to Poona. No problem. Only he is to make one stop on the way, at our home."

My stomach sinks. This guy has given private instructions, it was two something o'clock in the morning in a third world country, and our lives, passports and money are to be taken to some alley – and I am not coping. We have already paid. I look to Gimpy. No response.

I take nice-clothes aside and say to him, "Sir, I was going to leave this until later in my trip but perhaps you can help me. I am hoping to take back to Australia a large amount of best quality LSD. Maybe you can supply? No speed. LSD only."

A large grin comes to his face.

"Yes, no problem. I do cash deal only, sir. Do you have cash?"

I relax. This is where I want to be.

"Yes, but not with me, sir. I will be collecting $10,000 US dollars this week from my partner who is in Poona, waiting for me."

I watch him spin out internally.

"When can you return, sir?"

My voice lowered, and counting points on my fingers I say, "Wait! I want samples and we will try together before I buy. I tell you for sure, I have had first-best LSD and if you bring me rubbish there will be trouble – see my friend here? Then, no sale."

We discuss the excellence of his contact and supplier and where I will find him next week. Then he goes to his brother and speaks at length. The longer they talk the louder they yell. Suddenly it is over and we are in the van and off.

A while later, Kamala, in the back with Gimpy, says to him, "See? This is not so bad. Better than being stuck in Bombay all night."

"Oh, I like Bombay," said Gimpy. She is quiet after that, but squeaks as the van turns sharply to the right, away from the nuclear power plant, and up a dark alley.

"Where are you going sir?" I have not spoken to the driver since we got in and am surprised at the perfection of his English. "A short stop, sir. Only to deliver a message from my brother."

I look at his face. He is angry.

"How far?" I snap.

"Two hundred yards only, sir." I grab the handbrake, pull it hard, and skid the van to a stop under a streetlight.

"Good!" I say. "You walk from here, two hundred yards only, deliver the message and return. OKAY?"

He doesn't argue, gets out, leaves the motor running and jogs away. I get in the driver's seat and turn the bus around after he is out of sight. Kamala wants to know "what the fuck is going on?" Gimpy tells her, "Look... wait. We're probably not going to die now."

I love him. He knew all the time, said nothing and left me with it. I tell them of the farcical drug arrangement, the ten grand the elder brother is now waiting for and that I suspect the driver is now informing the hard men to wait for a week and there will be heaps more money than they would have had tonight.

I notice that Gimpy has his new torch in his hand. He bought the larger size. I turn back to the front, see that the driver has returned and is almost at the door. He is alone so

I slip back into the passenger seat.

When he is in and we have driven away, I hear the sound of the torch going into the pack and the zipper being done up. Turning, I notice that Kamala is very pale. I am totally unsympathetic. Good! I have been terrified throughout the entire episode. Gimpy slouches down and goes to sleep. I can't.

After miles of Bombay slum suburbia we begin to climb into the mountains, with unbelievable traffic and cliff edges. Suddenly we hit a monumental hole in the road, the back door flies open and all the van lights go out. Ross flies into the space behind the seat, grabs the luggage and pulls the doors shut. The driver hasn't even slowed down.

Again I am not coping. "Hey man, STOP!" I am verging on hysteria.

He turns to me and says, "It is okay. I can see very well."

He seems to have not noticed the rear door opening at all. We have already taken a break after Gimpy prodded him awake at the wheel several times, and he has come out of a sort of truck stop from hell, very awake and confident indeed. I have no idea what he can see, but I doubt that it has much to do with what *I* see, which is almost nothing.

I make him stop and we all take turns to play with wires in candlelight, until the lights come on. Two minutes later it begins to rain. Real rain, the tail end of the monsoon. Visibility zero.

I say to the driver, "Please sir, put the windscreen wipers on."

He tells me that they don't work, but "it is okay as he can see very well". I realise that I am in some form or other going to do this trip with a blinded driver, so I shut my eyes and try to sleep.

Gimpy wakes me later with a prod through the back of the seat and tells me that we are coming into Poona, and that I have missed two more truck stops that have made the driver very aware. Kamala is giving directions to the flat of a friend of hers where we could wake him up and stay.

"What time is it?" I ask.

"Around five."

I lose it. This is too much. "Look Kamala! This whole poxy episode has been to slake your desperate need to see someone ten hours earlier than we could have done it in comfort. There is no way I'm going to piss some stranger off by waking him up at five AM in demand of a bit of cold floor to sleep on, have stiff joints when I wake up, then get shitty food instead of breakfast. First we go to the Blue Diamond Hotel, I book into a room, and you can do what you like."

I feel better. I am going to my hotel room at last. I tell the driver to take us to the Blue Diamond. He knows where to go. It is a top end, well-known hotel. Kamala asks Ross what he is going to do, and he says he would rather sleep in a hotel room. She gets pissed off. "You two didn't have to come. You might as well have stayed in Bombay."

I don't know how to deal with this. She is right. I would rather have not come; I just didn't have the bottle to bail out, and that's not *her* fault.

I'm not confused for long, though, as Gimpy says, "He's a wimp. I don't care much what I do, but where do you think you would be now, if we hadn't come? Anyway, my back is fucked and I want a hot shower." She shuts up and I manage to get past that without taking any responsibility for my part in it.

At the hotel, we book in, and a young man in a turban and matching khaki uniform takes our luggage upstairs. The driver has demanded an extra payment for himself. I give him a hundred rupees and he curses me in Hindi. I think he is going to throw the money away, he is so angry.

I go back inside and follow my luggage up to the room,

where I find Kamala in tears on the bed. She has been on the telephone to the rich lover and been told in no uncertain terms by his parents that she is not welcome. We have all been around India long enough to know that she would be risking life and limb if she went there. Ross is in the shower already, so I am left to deal with this without him. I am pissed off. All this aggravating bullshit for a failing love affair.

I turn to Kamala...shit, she looks miserable. A wave of release comes on me and I am left feeling very sad for her. She is almost at the end of her professional life, not so cute anymore; and has made no provision for this part of her life at all. She has seen this guy as a way through the dark – and now nothing. She might really be in love with him as well. She is in serious strife.

I hug her, say I am really sorry, and send for coffee and breakfast. Ross comes out of the shower and I bring him up to date. We eat, and hold Kamala's hand for about an hour in between her convulsive tears. As soon as she can she calls a taxi and leaves.

"Jesus, Gimps," I say. "What's real here? I hated her two hours ago, then I was really sad, now I am just tired."

He laughs. "We live bullshit all the time, mate. Just stop thinking about it and get some sleep. You look bloody terrible."

# BROTHER PETER AND THE SACRED CANDLE

*Even when an ethos is rejected, it may still be in charge of life through your own need to avoid doing anything from that place. Although things as possessions were thought to be unimportant and even disadvantageous to clarity of consciousness, that was just more thinking. Desired or despised, things were still in charge.*

*I* am the best man at Peter's wedding. I was thrilled to be asked and unhesitating to accept. He is my most ancient brother.

We shared the Sixties house together. In those years our lives spun madly through great experiments in consciousness, vast and deeply scarring loves, very good food indeed and the compressed evolution of about a thousand lifetimes.

The food here is less holy and the prevalent ideological base is certainly one of self-indulgence. I am, however, no less at home.

Peter has made a great deal of money and is spending lots of it tonight. We are sitting in some sort of beach resort conference room; lots of people, a great bar in the corner, live music, unbelievable wine list. His new drug of choice is fine wine.

I am feeling easy when I focus on either of my knowings of Peter, but am having a bit of an integration problem with the both together. I have a speech coming up. I will address the problem then. I am under some pressure to give Peter the proper traditional amount of stick during this time and I'm not sure if I can do it. I'm a little drunk, so I might.

We had champagne of greatness in the limo on the way here. I was thirsty and unaware with the first glass and didn't smell or care for it at all well; just drank it. Then wine with the meal. All wonderful.

Speeches are continuing – me soon. I made notes and have them in my pocket.

I look at Peter, in a tux. He has a perfect command of all this, at ease and at home. I did my first acid with this man and it was a good choice. I might say that as a comment of praise in the speech – a few people here will know how that ties you together. I see both families; Peter's proper earthsalt workers from the Port, Maree's from a more comfortable and middle-class place. And at the edge, a table of Peter's mildly demented friends.

I hear my name and automatically separate a little from my body. I am at this point only to thank the bridesmaids. Anecdotal jollity has been formally slotted in at the end, after all the proper speeches.

Up to the rostrum and into it. Encouragement from the demented table.

A microphone. "Settle. You're not at the football!"

More noise. I surf. "I know that I am only thanking the bridesmaids at this point, but…,"

Drunken applause, loud shouts of "Yes!"

"… there are some things that in the name of responsible behaviour I really should tell Maree."

Notes out of the tux pocket and a deep breath. "I first met Peter in the late Sixties. We did a meditation course together, then shared a house with thousands of other people. It was a proper Sixties house, and we did all the things that our parents thought we might."

Shit. I hate making it all sound trite and – ha ha – adolescent silliness that I have grown out of. Lots of people I know from then do this. I'm convinced that it is a mechanism for denying the disappointment that it proved to be too difficult to make manifest the love into the world.

"Peter was great. He had work, so we all felt secure about the rent, and he had stuff. A car, a bike, furniture, even cooking stuff – thanks to Betty."

Betty is Peter's mother, a tiny madwoman whose fame stems from ejecting a serious bunch of bikers, the Gypsy Jokers, from a party, with shrieks and a broom. A good girl, Betty; older now, but still fast.

"Anyway, Peter proved to be a wonderful person to share with. Generous, and in the spirit of the times, not attached to his possessions."

You had no choice, really. It was the dominant ethic of the day. Be easy, or be straight.

"I already mentioned the car and bike, but what he loved most was his candle. It was just beautiful; huge, a metre tall and hand-dripped to make a beautiful, complex, woven, wax sculpture. During a black period of his early adolescence he had stayed in his room for about a year, melted wax and dropped it by hand on this thing. I could see when he carried it into the house that it was worth more than his life."

I have sensibly brought my drink and now stop to drain the glass for emphasis.

"A few weeks passed and on a lovely spring day I borrowed his bike to ferry a mate to his house in the hills. We had travelled only a mile, and, due entirely to the oil leaking from the front forks and the consequent absence of front brakes, I crashed it good. I went home terrified."

Rightly so, I thought at the time. Peter had made an ex-Police BSA A65 into this beautiful thing with big dollar paint, custom pipes and the very hot motor. And I had used it to fold a car in half with. Thankfully I had sprained my wrist and had a very fine sling and bandage to defend myself with.

"No need of course. When I arrived home, Peter said that it was fine, man, and was I okay?"

I wave my glass, and someone from the fringe table fills it. I drink again. This performance business is great!

"Later, Robby, a mechanic of extremely dubious ideology who lived in the front sty, went out in Peter's car – a nice little sports coupe Fiat – and he put *that* into the safety rails of the freeway. Peter said, that was fine, man, and was he okay?

"Life went on easy for a while, until one night a couple of friends and I partied into the night. We were well away at about ten, when we decided to light the candle."

I am screaming to tell the truth here. That was the night of the first acid I had ever had with speed in it. This made a silent, gentle and introverted drug experience into a manic twistout. We couldn't sit still or stay quiet; the speed made it impossible to turn attention inwards so we had to do things and sit just under the surface of our consciousness. The whole thing was the start of the tragic end of the Sixties, although we didn't know that then – we thought we would easily find pure acid again. The Sandoz Company was still making it, after all.

I don't see an easy way to say this to the collected relatives. Better they assume we were drunk, ha ha.

"The next morning we were still sitting about when Peter surfaced to go to work and came into the room, to see the once majestic candle reduced to a wine bottle in a pool of wax. He looked a little crestfallen, then said, 'Oh. You lit the candle.'

"I felt bad and started to speak, but when he turned to listen, he saw my condition, interrupted me and said, 'That's fine, man – are you okay?'"

The crowd is learning by repetition here, grinning at the caring; and the laughter is louder each time Peter is reported to have lost something and not minded. What to do with it now? Lie as planned I suppose, or the speech will have no credibility.

"Years later – only a week ago, in fact – we were drinking to celebrate his impending wedding and I reminded him of his deep loving nature, as I have you; and with amazing speed for one so old, his hand took my shirt front, and with his face very close to mine, he said through clenched teeth that he had always hated us for that, and always wanted to tell us how it all had pissed him right off."

Peter and I both know the truth here and I am cringing inside as it is sold down the tube for the sake of social form.

He had said in response to my reminder that it had all hurt a bit and therefore he wasn't sure that it was selflessness but, more likely, adherence to social form. Then we had a long rave about that and concluded that we were tied to performance standards as rigid as those in the straight world and that even though they were more humane, slavery is slavery. Sad.

Back to the speech.

"I was very shaken at that point, but I pushed myself away, brushed my shirt flat and said in my best loud voice, 'Get back into your room and make yourself another candle!' But I didn't respond in kind, I'm not that sort of person. Instead, I decided to tell on him. So now I have.

"Maree, the advice I have for you is that when all is well, in particular when you are amazed at Peter's tolerance and equanimity in the face of material loss, just you wait. Thirty years later the mongrel will have his hand around your throat and be hissing shocking abuse at your very essence. My advice is, in twenty-nine years, just leave him. Don't wait for it."

Much falling about is happening. The demented table has seen Peter suffer, and the straight relatives have a tale from a couple of good old lads grown out of it and settled down. The only casualty is the truth. I thank the bridesmaids and sit.

I don't feel much angst about straying from the truth – this is a wedding speech for God's sake – just the feeling that some things in your life ought not to be rendered unto Caesar, as they are the blocks you stand on. Peter and I come from a gentle and positive time, a gifted adolescence with space to seek and find. It did not include the kind of violence I have spoken of. So I feel a bit like a traitor to my roots.

About to turn to Peter with an apology, I feel a hand on my shoulder and turn with a start – to find him standing beside me about to speak.

"Relax, bro, I love you. I know who you are."

# ROLEX IN INDIA

*We all go along planting in each moment the seeds*
*of the future. I have no idea what effect I am having,*
*nor, it seems, does anyone else.*
*But once, I changed people's lives forever.*

*I* knew something different was happening on the way to
breakfast when a stranger threw purple dye at me, laughed
a lot, and ran off. I stood, looking down at my clothes in
astonishment.

India is a place of tremendous sensory impact and bizarre
events are frequent. That in itself wouldn't be too much to
take, but the vast amount of sense-battering information
simply doesn't fit together in any comfortable way. This purple dye on my clothes was disturbingly out of any context I
knew.

"It's Holi, sir," said the man passing on a bicycle, as if he
had explained everything. I laughed and said, "Of course
sir, I had forgotten," He laughed too and pedalled furiously
away.

India has holidays, lots of them, all relating to gods, gurus
and seasons. Holi, I discovered later, is a harvest thanksgiv-
ing festival. A celebration whose public face is now mainly
young men catharting their repressed sexuality (in the name
of gratitude for fecundity) at all and sundry for this one day.
They are aided in this by betel-nut, hash, speed and whatever cocktail sold with the name of LSD that young Mohan
on the corner puts together.

I see the point of the exercise. Being a citizen of India has to be a particularly bloody flavour of hell nowadays and you would have to let it all out in some way; but I got caught in it, and like an ignorant foreigner did all the wrong things, to be rescued only at the last moment by some great omnipresent Pythonesque God.

I was in Poona, an ex-British hill station up the road from Bombay, famous for being the birthplace of Spike Milligan and, more recently, for containing the Rajneesh Ashram.

I was visiting the Ashram, listening to him talk most nights, eating out, meditating and doing all the right things for a fine few months in India. If I had been on a tour, or involved in life a bit more directly, I would have heard that there was a festival, got information, a guide, something.

I ate breakfast with an American woman, Madhuria, a delightful, quietly intelligent woman who had been a friend for several years. She looked a bit like Carole King, wearing cheesecloth and the entire American-in-India comfort gear. She was interested in everything, so we decided to have an in-town Holi explore, after lunch.

I was insulated from India all that morning – meditation, talking, coffee, reading, then eating lunch at the buffet that the Ashram does so beautifully. I took salad, pizza and chai, and sat down in the garden feeling positively eclectic, when I saw the black guy again.

India can stress you in a million ways, but their bank's favourite is to swallow your money when it arrives from home. This guy clearly had more money than God. 'Real Estate' he said; I had my doubts. He kept calling me 'man'.

He saw me, came up and asked to buy his watch back from me. We had been through this three or four times since his money had arrived, so I said, "No, man, let's not do it again."

"Shit man, you stole that from me."

Completely forgetting my resolve not to enter the arena,

I said, "No, I *didn't*, man. You sold it to me last week. I really like it, and I'm going to keep it. OKAY?"

He was grinning now. Having placed bait and scored well, he went on, "I was in the shit last week and I'm okay now. Look! I'll give you six hundred bucks."

For three weeks, the Bank of India had mucked this guy around for his American dollars. He was totally lost in the adventure of his first time here, got really poor and sold me his Rolex for $500.00 U.S. I didn't think he would take it, but although he was truly rich, he was hungry and in tight times. He revalued it, I bought it, and now we played this "sell it back" game whenever we met.

I knew it was genuine, because every time I wore it outside the Ashram, Indians wandered up to me wanting to buy it. They never miss. If it was a fake they would have known at any distance. I had never had a rich man's watch before and my plan was to keep it forever, give it to my kids, or something of the sort.

"Hey, it's not for sale! I love it; I won't ever get another one. Let's just drop it, man, it's not going to happen." He laughed, smacked me on the shoulder, and left.

I felt good. I usually do whatever anybody else wants. I spent the next few minutes drinking the tea and thinking that the meditations must be working.

I caught a rickshaw to the café up the road where I was to meet Madhuria. There was definitely an 'up' sort of mood about. Purple spots on the rickshaw driver – he must know about this, so I asked him.

"What is happening today, sir?"

I always get the feeling that all Indians hate all westerners because we are, just by flying into the country, wealthy beyond their dreams. So I call the men 'sir'. It seems tacky, but the British showed them no respect, and by and large they deserve some.

Ignoring the oncoming traffic, he turned round to face me, grinned, and said with wobbling head, "It is Holi, sir. Big holy day, everybody is in a party."

I thought that if I wanted more information than this I really should buy a book. At the café, Madhuria was in white, looking really clean, and no purple spots. I had changed into older local clothes, to not mind the colouring I was bound to get. She had heard that it was water-soluble dye and would wash out. Since Indian dye washes out in everything else, I figured it was probably true. She laughed, we jumped in the rickshaw and headed for MG (Mahatma Gandhi) Road.

There were big crowds in the road – mad, shouting, moving everywhere at once. Smelly, purple, arms around each other; men in groups, women scurrying.

We jumped out and I could feel myself vanish. This is why I love India. The doing of it is magic. Totally foreign, not one cue to follow, no way to predict even the next second. The idea of self from your own culture has no place here so it simply disappears, my total foreign-ness bringing the witness. Separate, the same, watching, empty; it's just heaven. We flowed in and about, getting more purple, more wet. I was well content when Madhuria shrieked, and jumped toward me.

She was not having a good time. I've known her for an age. She is an old hand at India management and this stuff just doesn't bother her, so I asked, "Hey, what's happening?" thinking she must be suddenly sick; but not so.

"Everybody keeps grabbing me and feeling me up."

There were tears coming. She was frightened. It was time to leave. Holding her hand I turned to find no rickshaw, heard her scream hugely, and felt her hand twist away. Looking back, I saw a young Indian guy grabbing her top and pulling.

I couldn't believe it! Without hesitation I dived forward and knocked him over with my body. I'm big so he sat straight down in the dust. Standing between Madhuria and him, I noted his eyes. He was well out of it and very pissed off. He pushed himself up with his already clenched fists and raised his hands to fight. I didn't mind. I had been irregularly training in a Chinese martial art for almost ten years. I could surely sit him on his bum again and go.

Madhuria screamed again. Louder and terrible this time – not uncomfortable, but terrified. Looking around us, a space already made and the circle forming, the faces showed me the proof of my hate theory. All red eyes, bamboo sticks and sneering grins, it was beat the foreign intruder time. I was petrified. Christ! I didn't want to die.

In panic I looked around, saw a gap and (there *is* a God!) a bloody rickshaw. With the speed only fear can give, I grabbed Madhuria's arm and bolted through the gap, leaving the boys all standing flat-footed due to drug time delay.

I looked up at the rickshaw and my heart sank. The driver was just a kid and had no interest in us. He was sitting back with his feet on the scooter handlebars, arms folded, shaking his head.

The noise of pursuit started behind us. We were dead, and we knew it. At certain moments in life there is a greater consciousness that responds to the intensity of a situation, that just takes over your body and acts – something truly ancient that sits back, watching, and steps up in crisis to take over. It's only happened to me a couple of times, but there is no denying its reality or power.

I watched from some internal distance as my left arm lifted and my right hand pointed, first at my watch and then at the rickshaw driver.

The noise came back. I gaped at the rickshaw guy, who turned into St. George, started the rickshaw and, greeting us with, "Come sir, I will help you", pushed his foot into someone's chest. Madhuria and me were already in the back, and all three of us shoved the youth of India off the side of our steed and bolted away, laughter behind us.

I looked at Madhuria. She was very shaken.

I'm sure Americans feel this cultural aggression very deeply, just because they are so relaxed in the vast power of their country. Hugs and tears; then a wash and drink from the water bottle in my backpack. We started to relax a bit, gave the driver the address of my flat and sat back.

Now, I am an honourable man, but the only reason that I didn't pay this guy a hundred bucks instead of the watch was because the watch was offered to him from somewhere beyond my doing. Ignoring these inputs would be just stupid.

We were both settled when we arrived outside my place, and we realised that the driver had no real idea what he was getting. He refused to believe that a watch could be worth thousands of American dollars. Our dilemma was that some sharp operator would without doubt take it from him and give him a few rupees.

So, off again; this time to the black market change place at the back of the jewellery shop. As we all went in, the security lads were down on the rickshaw driver straight away. He was nervous in the place – it was quite uncomfortable. These were seriously dangerous operators who the original owner of the watch wouldn't go near.

Madhuria said she would take the driver outside to wait in the rickshaw, because she figured he would be beaten and robbed moments after he was alone with the money. She was right, of course. India is reasonably kind to foreigners, but shows no mercy to its own in matters of wealth distribution.

I sold the watch. Four thousand American dollars in rupees. I was tremendously impressed that the guy had it in the drawer. I tried to count it twice, with everybody laughing. No-one can count notes like a moneychanger in India.

I was a regular customer so I was unlikely to be ripped

off, particularly since I was clearly a rich man selling a Rolex. Finally, I left without counting.

Outside, with two plastic bags bursting with bundles of rupees, one hundred and twenty thousand. Into the rickshaw and up to my flat.

The rickshaw driver, poor kid, was in culture shock. He'd been in a rescue, inside the inner sanctums of the black market, and was now inside a westerner's beautiful flat, finding himself with an unbelievable amount of money. He quite reasonably burst into tears. I put the money in a sports bag and made tea for us all. We drank. He settled down a bit.

As he left, after much foot touching and thanks, he turned to us and said, "Can I drive you somewhere again tomorrow, please?"

We thought probably not.

I never saw him again, but on asking when I came again the next year, an old rickshaw driver remembered young Akhbar suddenly going to Bombay with his whole extended family. Then a story coming later, of them having a room and a new, 'Not reconditioned sir, brand new!' rickshaw running full-time as the family business.

I hope it's true.

# SHORT GRUMPY CONVERSATION WITH A POST-MODERNIST KIDDIE

*I treasure what I believe in, just like everyone else, and like them I will defend it with surprising brutality. You never know what is inside until you are pushed.*

*I* like to drink coffee. As with any drug I like it both as best quality and in its purest form, so I inhabit a nice inner city coffee shop a couple of mornings a week.

This day Nathan joins me. He is a friend of one of my 'not quite' children, the ones you inherit when you live with their mother. He is around 20, cynical and sharp. He has always been a smoker in my memory and we have raved at length. I find his new haircut disturbing. He sits and asks after my health.

"I'm fine man. You?"

He leans back.

"Yeah, just great."

We talk about his efforts to get work; and his new girl-friend. She's pregnant, he doesn't mind. His separated parents are both academics with a nice share portfolio and he is supplied money in quantity without aggravation. All goes well until he asks what I am doing. I tell him that I have paid for my house in the hills and am going to teach computing this year. I am staggered by his reply.

"Another baby boomer hippie selling out and getting into the system – what happened to the revolution?"

I think he's joking and look up to see that he looks a bit

adversarial, so I try to go sideways.

"Shit, Nathan, it's only a place to live."

He's not joking and he's not going to ease up. He's onto something that has pissed him off and is going to get into me.

"No it's not – it's typical of your generation; getting nice things all of a sudden when you inherit, moving into all the power positions, doing all the stuff that used to turn your stomach as if it all doesn't go against everything you say you stand for."

I am totally astonished. This is not a position I think I should need to defend. He is leaning forward now, looking aggrieved and punchy. I say in my mellow voice, "Nathan, I don't think I ought be called the middle-class oppressor of all things alternative because I own a house."

"And are teaching inside a corrupt system, supporting an education system that is abusing kids and nothing bloody else."

This all sounds familiar to me, as I said it a lot a while ago.

"What's up your arse today, man? I just live somewhere and have a part-time job so I can eat and keep my trip together."

"Bullshit, man! You used to tell me and Andrew that the interior of a person is of primary consequence and the rest is secondary. I look around and am being fucked over by all your mates who are now taking a turn at being old and in the way."

In a very real sense Nathan is right. I think of Peter, full -time accruing wealth and surrounded by people whom we both used to smoke and trip with, also doing a money trip for their old age. That's it of course. We are unable to keep our activities politically sound, as our bodies can't cut it any-more.

"Listen, Nathan. It's still true as far as I'm concerned; take good care of your innards and that's the main game played.

The thing that is different for me now is that, unlike you, I have a new chemical job descriptor. I can't rough it now. I need to take care of the outer stuff in a new way because I have to sit down and rest more often."

"Then go and sit down, and not hang on to the power like the parents you hated. Anyway, if the spiritual rave isn't true for you now, then it wasn't true for you then and so isn't true for anyone ever. That stuff should be an absolute or it is wrong. You fucked up. Go away and let us do it right."

I press my idea further. "Look, man, you have a young person's job. Mainly it's to abuse older people and give them shit about the state of things. I did it and now it's your turn. And you are doing it very nicely, thank you. Later you will get older and want to sit and drink coffee. Someone will come and give you shit about all the stuff you inherit, earn, or do and fuck your day up. You will think it's well over the top and wish they would stop."

Red rag to a bull at this point, if I remember rightly. The implication that the current opinion of youth is not cast in stone and might well change someday will shake Nathan and probably piss him off even further. I should remind him that he once loved Michael Jackson with this fervour and one-pointedness. Better not. He still doesn't look happy.

"That's just bullshit and you know it, you tricky old bastard. Real is real. You can't take the pace anymore because what you believed is bullshit and what you are doing to get by now is bullshit too. I've got my material trip sorted already and will keep it that way. You lot are now being corporate arseholes and ideological dinosaurs. We will get you and all your hippie crap out of our way any minute now and you can rot on your patch of decaying nonsense."

Jesus, what is happening here? This is very heavy and I'm getting pissed off. This bugger has no idea of who I am and is measuring it against some stance that is totally foreign to me. So I am now shitty.

"Nathan, I know you have your money trip together, and I remember the people who are doing it for you. Both baby boomers as I recall. How *are* your mum and dad?"

He stands, reaches into his bag and brings out a wad of large bills that would definitely not fit into his pocket and spits, "I'm doing very well in the real world without them or their trickle of emotionally charged assistance, so you fell on your arse, man."

He sits down again. I detect an air of finality. Such a lot of money. I choose to not wonder where he got it from – even his parents were not this generous. I am now properly offside, and my little 'sitting, drinking and watching' ritual is shattered. Nathan has called me names, but what really cuts me up is that he sneered when he called me 'man'. I notice that my teeth are clenched and lips tight. I lean forward and speak.

"Nathan, you have no fucking idea what is going on inside me. I have come from another planet to be here. Let me tell you about it. It had lots of trees, lots of hope, less than half the number of people that are on this one and there was a spirit of generosity you cannot imagine. We hitchhiked without fear, sex couldn't kill you, the sun was friendly and there were jobs everywhere. We didn't live in the fear of losing our souls, we didn't hate anyone and we didn't abuse people in coffee shops. Let's see you go and fucking buy that, you grumpy little shit."

I leave. The sun is still shining, not yellow and mellow like where I came from, but still nice to be in for a while.

# ON SELLING MY CAR

*Once, for a moment, all the crap was
discovered to be diamonds.
After that, of course, you're buggered when it changes back.*

*I* have placed an advertisement in today's paper and am waiting for calls. I used Ross's phone number as I live away from the city and people won't come so far to inspect a used car. I got this one as repayment of a debt. It's a monster Chrysler with a 5.1 litre motor. Thank God it's in good condition; nobody likes a petrol guzzler now except the good old boys.

I stayed at Ross's last night and we spent much of the night bullshitting. He is an insightful bugger and kept cracking up whenever I mentioned selling the Chrysler.

"You have sold more cars than Henry bloody Ford, mate. You get them, do them up and just when they are right, you piss them off."

It's true.

"I get bored with them, mate; I like to fiddle."

He wasn't having any. "Gimpy, there's more to it than that. I'm stuffed if I know. I figure that it's some kind of disease you've got and there is no cure. Still, I always look forward to a ride in your new car every couple of weeks."

The night went on as usual. We went out to drink coffee and eat chocolate mousse, late, and started talking at length about the declining quality of drugs. How dope once had regional names that defined its qualities. We conjured images with words like 'Acapulco gold' and 'Durban poison', then went on to note the bodily nature of the effect that Indian hashish had as opposed to the heady nature of Moroccan.

Ross had never taken any acid; rather he was a big smoker at the time of our youth, and so acid stories were less interactive but welcomed. I told my favourite, the one I always tell.

"When you could get acid pure, mate, the only way it was worth taking, I had paid a few dollars to a psychiatric nurse to find me some in their medicine cupboard. When it arrived at my place, I was alone. The woman who brought it couldn't stay so I took 500 microgrammes of pure Sandoz on my own."

"What's Sandoz?" Ross interjected.

"It's the name of a chemical company in Sweden or Switzerland. They made LSD."

"I've got a mate who used to make LSD."

"Not like this, man. Pure, it is a slut of a chemical, unstable as buggery and wants to combine with almost everything that moves. Sandoz acid used to come in a little bottle with a rubber cap that you could stick a syringe through and suck it out. They filled the space in the top of the bottle with Nitrogen so that it was stable until you got it, and the trip was seamless. No aggravation on the way up or back. Sitting silently going in, watching the stuff you are made of unfold."

The waitress came, bringing all the goodies. Ross thanked her for coming, as I am 'a boring bastard who talks too much'. She smiled at him and retired fairly quickly.

Undeterred, I continued. "Anyway, after I swallowed it I sat on the lounge chair to wait. Soon I was seeing more colour, then moving inward. I was convinced at the time that nothing existed. I still am, but it doesn't seem to matter much now."

I looked at Ross. He had mousse in his moustache, but he looked interested, so I assumed he was and went straight on.

"Sometime later I was watching pictures come and go, and I thought, well, they don't exist either. As soon as I thought that, the current picture just went away. I kept this up for a while and stuff just came and went."

I lit up a cigarette. God, I wish I had never started smoking; it's the worst drug I have ever had anything to do with. Every time I stop I want to kill things. A woman I know stopped being a junkie when she found out she was pregnant and is still managing quite well, yet she smokes 20 cigarettes a day and tells me that there is no way that she can stop. We will both die of it if we don't.

Ross was looking at me, shaking his head with apparent concern. I stopped musing and resumed my story. "I was losing interest when I noticed two things. First, that once a picture had gone it didn't come back. Also, the longer I did this, the more archetypal the pictures became. The crone, the devil, the wise old man, cave, all came and went. After some time, it seemed about twenty minutes, there was nothing left. No more pictures came. Shit, I felt quiet."

"What, you reckon you emptied your head out?"

"I don't know, mate, but it must have been nearly empty because when I opened my eyes there were no names for anything, unless I sort of wanted them; then they came. I couldn't believe it. Just vision, all clear and empty – things existing without overlay of preconception. Just there. I wasn't scared, just silent; so, I decided to go outside and have a look around. My body was there – a little distant – but very there. This was different to the usual acid experience, working around the inside of my head, sitting and seeing. This was beyond all that stuff."

I felt my chest quiver and my breath shorten. I knew that if I looked, I would find my hands shaking. These things always happen when I talk about this. Ross noticed, but made no comment.

"When I opened the door and went into the street, another bit came. There were still no names or judgment, but now it was all moving, and so very bright! I was so full. Walking, talking, just looking; it was all the same. Silent and loud all at once. I loved it. After a while, I could feel a really big, broad sensation across my chest. My breath became shallower and my legs loosened; then a bubble popped inside of me and moved outwards, gently filling every space with a sort of kindness. There was a lot of space, mate, because all the stuff had been moved out of my head."

Ross looked impressed; we had heard enough talk from Indian gurus to have a hint of where I might have been.

"Shit, man, I know why they call it bliss."

I could feel tears ready to show. I ate mousse and drank coffee. The sense of loss passed and I went on, "The bliss didn't stop, mate. It just kept going, and going, outward forever. I realised I had come home. It was all over. I would never leave here. My life was to be nothing more or less than eternal, infinite bliss. Just like all the holy men had said."

Ross hadn't eaten for a while and the drinks were getting cold. I was just about shipwrecked, but said the obvious.

"It went on and on. The next thing I remember that was different, was weeping in the shower the next morning, wanting my body to wash off. Shit, it was heavy."

"The scene or your body?"

"Both, mate. I don't remember how or when it came unstuck, just that it had. Fuck, I wish it hadn't."

I sat, a bit miserable. Ross ate, and was obviously sympathetic. I assumed he didn't know what it all meant to me or what to say about it, but realised I was quite wrong when he looked up at me and quietly said, "Shit, you poor bastard! No wonder you can't decide which car to keep."

# KOMBI GOTHIC

*We all need an old friend or two to help us through.*

"*I* had forgotten how seriously uncomfortable these are."

This from my old mate Neil, a once famous Volkswagen guru, now middle-aged and a bit cynical about his hippie past.

We are driving on a dirt road in a 1964 VW Kombi as run by one of the current crop of what I internally call neo-hippies. The van delights me. It has been painted with a brush, pastel green bottom half, and purple top. The stripe in the middle is white with a bright green, Celtic-style graphic all round. I think Neil would be embarrassed if anyone were out here.

Supposedly we are looking for the solution to a fault that is driving the youthful owner nuts. The generator light never quite goes out. I am driving.

"You know, these are the only vehicles I know of that the driver can safely roll a joint in while you're going along."

The steering wheel is huge and sits flat like a proper little bus.

Neil is not impressed. "The anaesthetic effect is critical to being in here for more than five minutes." He goes on to postulate that as the only real reason for their hippie popularity.

We both know what is wrong with the van. It has to do with the distance between the electrical action at the rear near the motor and the light at the front. We also know there is no harm in it and the traditional solution is to paint the offending light with fingernail polish or something you can't quite see through. So if that is the case, I wonder out loud, why is he a co-operative participant in this afternoon's unnecessary activity?

We are going to a country pub in Michael's Kombi and he isn't expecting it back until evening. "I dunno, mate, I must be mad."

I can't help loudly noticing that the steering and brakes are both in need of attention. Gear stick is loose too.

"And it's bloody noisy in here. The thing's got more rattles than a millionaire's baby."

I have brought with me several tapes that will complete the period piece we are doing and slip one into the stereo. Van Morrison starts at proper volume, *"She's as sweet as Tupelo honey."* Something I hadn't even recognised as tension relaxes in me. This is good. I can't quite understand what is happening with Neil. Some of the Sixties don't travel well to the present, but he seems to look at it all as though he was a cynical outsider. I begin to sing along with the tape.

*"She's an angel of the first degree...."*

In fact he is deeply involved in the caring ethic and together we have returned many Volkswagens to the world for almost no financial reward. I must ask him about this.

We are coming up to the pub that is destined to have us sit in it for the next hour. It has Guinness on tap and a beer garden with a view of a nice little creek. Great place. I press hard on the brakes long before it could possibly be needed and just manage to slow down enough to slew into the car park of the Brothers Hotel.

I turn off the car. Van Morrison dies, the tape spits out, and after running on a bit, the motor stops too.

"These things are getting old," I say. "Almost dangerous in today's terms."

"Definitely, I'd say," replies Neil, with some panic in the voice I think. "Let's have Guinness."

We can't lock the van, so we decide to trust existence and go to the bar and order a half of Guinness each. As we wait Neil reminds me of an old girlfriend of his whose van also wouldn't lock, so whenever she parked it, she thought a pyramid over it.

"Did it ever get stolen?"

"No."

I think that is at least proof of the possibility of it being effective, but Neil isn't having any.

"She was a head case, man, all sweet and easy, but her mind was like a can of worms. I never met anyone who could avoid responsibility for what she did as well as her. Not even you." I'm not hurt.

The Guinness has arrived. We take it out the back, avoid all the umbrellas and sit under the tree. I put my feet up on an empty chair.

I remember Chrissie. She was little and pretty, big round glasses and long brown hair. Cute. She'd lived with Neil for a long time, went to a course in some healing thing and left him for someone else straight after. It pissed him right off. Not because she left, but that it came to light in the break-up administration that she had been going with this guy for a couple of years yet saw no reason to say anything to Neil. Her Kombi was nice, though. When I say so to Neil, he reminds me of its birth.

"You sold that to me. You only had it for a couple of weeks and it was the wrong body type for you. It had two sets of double doors in the back."

"Oh, that bloody thing. It wasn't the doors. I got rid of it because of all the letters."

Only a couple of days after I had registered it in my name, I started getting weird mail from someone's insurance company claiming that one morning I had driven over his toe. Further, that he had consequently lost his job and might I be interested in compensating Mr. Victim for his trauma and loss? I decided to sell it because at the time I wanted nothing to do with heavy vehicle karma. I had never explained this to Neil. He seems pleased when I tell him now.

"That explains the guy coming up in the street to admire it after I'd fitted it out for Chrissie. A bent-looking bugger. He kept asking if I had any trouble with registration or the law. He was strangely reticent to explain and, when pressed, left at speed." This last sentence in a 'policeman at a press conference' voice.

"Ever see anyone limping towards you shaking their fist?"

"No." Neil leans back and stretches both arms out. "God, that whole trip fucked me right up." I think he means the van fit-out. The job he'd done was great. He's now a wood turner and always his woodwork was classy stuff. Chrissie had ended up with one of the nicest vans I'd seen.

"Why didn't you take it apart before she left?" I don't mean this, but want to offer some input that will elicit a response. It does.

"Not the van, you dumb bastard! All of it. I spent years putting in and ended up fucked over and cynical."

I think we might be getting close to the point. "It wasn't all like that – just the last bit, and that was only the last bit because you stopped putting in."

"I need a piss, I'll be back in a minute."

You know that feeling when you are driving, you get pulled over and are almost sure you've had one drink too many? I have it now. I should learn to shut up.

I look at the creek, drinking and noting that all my friends run to the toilet under stress. Neil comes back, working his way past a newly arrived group of bikers. Not the worrying sort; lawyers in leather and nice helmets. I imagine their bikes, like coloured peanuts in a row.

After he sits down Neil looks straight at me and says, "Look, mate, it was too hard then, and it's a bloody sight harder now."

I agree with the last bit. It is nearly impossible in these rationalist times to live gently and co-operatively. Every time I make the effort I end up feeling like I imagine indigenous people feel in their own country – ripped off. He is right. This is why lawyers can afford motorcycles; they are the shock troops of rationalism. There is no room in these crowded days for the confusing addition of emotions into the process of decision-making.

I begin to feel disenfranchised and sympathetic to Neil's thinking. "If it wasn't for my screen door, mate, I'd give it in."

"What, get a straight job?"

"Maybe."

Neil hesitates, squints and says, "What was that obtuse reference to your door?"

I have a beautiful wooden screen door at the front of my house. Although it only more or less keeps flies out and has no possible security function, it's a pretty thing. Neil had stripped the paint from it and we had installed it together.

I start, "When I was a kid..."

"Oh, fuck," says Neil, "a rave. I'll get another drink."

I have been Neil's mate for over thirty years and he has what an old carpenter would call a 'good eye'. But his insight goes further than this; he has the capacity to see the flaws in anything he pays attention to. It all gets hard for him when his good eye applies itself automatically to society and, in particular, his life. The results make him highly cynical about things most of us live with reasonably easily.

He returns. I notice he's got one Guinness and one Coke. I get the Guinness.

"Tell us about your door then." He sits back and puts his

legs back up on the opposite chair.

"When I was a kid, you rude bastard..." He smiles. It's a particular kind of old friend that enjoys abuse. "...we had an old screen door at the back of the house. The wire screen was broken and it had a hook to hold it shut in the wind. Every time we came home, we used that door, and for all the shit I got, I was safe inside, always enough to eat, and warm."

"Yeah, yeah, I know – home. Existential warm fuzzies. What are you talking about?"

"Wait! It made a noise that nothing else in the world makes, that type of twisted sprung hinges and the thing with rubber rollers that the door hits and then it holds the door shut, sort of squeeaak kerthwup. Okay?" He nods. Of course he knows the noise; all our age group do.

"Well, now I have one of my own and whenever I get home, I am made welcome by my roots. It's deep."

Neil is more interested than I thought he'd be. After a while he speaks.

"You could do that with all the vanished worlds we come from, couldn't you?"

"The ones that help. You choose. All you need is the symbol."

Pause. "You're a clever bastard."

We drink silently long enough for me to get paranoid about it. Finally Neil says, "Let's go."

We work our way through the bar and out to the car park. There is a row of high tech, pretty Japanese motorbikes and, a bit further up, one Harley. The bloke who owns the Harley is tying a pit-bull terrier to the front wheel of the first lawyer's bike. I wave and he sort of nods to me.

We get to the van and Neil stops at the driver's side door and asks me for the keys. He states that I have, in fact, drunk twice as much as him and should therefore allow him to drive. I give him the keys. As we build up speed he shakes the gear stick and says, "This poor baby does need help."

I begin to look forward to a new series of greasy days.

We sing along with Van Morrison all the way to my place and then I give Neil a packet of Symbolic brand incense to take him home to where he came from.

# JOHN THE RUNNER

*Fearlessly, the idiot faced the crowd. Smiling.*
Pink Floyd

*W*hen I opened the door there were two guys standing there. Both freaks – lots of hair, and clothes in lovely rainbow colours. The blonde one was scratching his eye through his glasses frame in the absence of a lens. They were nervous.

Glasses looked at my chest and said how he was sorry to bother us, but their car had a flat tyre and they didn't know what to do but had seen us working on our cars out the front and could we help them, please?

"Sure, man," I said. "Where is it?"

When Peter and I got to the car a few houses away there was no spare or jack, so we went back, picked up my trolley jack, took the tyre to be fixed, had a joint while we waited, then put the wheel back on the car.

Alison was the guy's name; his mate was called Rainbow. Alison had changed his name by deed poll from John to Alison Wonderland, apparently for the joy of replying, when asked by the police "Alison who?", "Alison Wonderland" – and skipping gaily away. It was about then that I figured out he might be a junkie.

After the tyre was fixed we went to our place for tea, then ate, smoked and raved the night away. Rainbow left early but Alison stayed on until very late.

Next day we didn't see him, but the day after he came with a heavily made-up black eye, drank tea, and when asked, explained how Rainbow had been jealous and so had thumped him when he belatedly arrived home. What he had come back for was more information about the poster that he had seen on our wall. Maharishi Mahesh Yogi featured on it with a quote about being and nature. Alison had liked his eyes and wanted more.

"He looks so beautiful, it makes me feel calm just to look at him."

I had seen this happen before. Maharishi was absolutely the archetypal Indian guru. People with the gap left by disenfranchisement or cultural rejection mostly aren't able just to live in the space left in your head when the old values fall. Enter the gentle, loving face of the Indian guru with the promise of belonging somewhere, combined with the moral high ground of seeking the final goal of enlightenment. It looks not so much like a lifeboat but the solid ground of the Holy Land.

And ... it very effectively fills the space left by the vanished old values. What a relief!

John (who had already asked us to call him John and not Alison) wanted to know more, so we told him. The standard, missionary style, full TM raves. Deep relaxation, stress release, ever-expanding consciousness. We could have said anything vaguely coherent. He was already a goner.

As fast as he could, John got his trip together to gather the TM prerequisites of flowers, fruit, money and a clean handkerchief. A week or so later he was dressed beautifully in cheesecloth shirt and loose trousers at the local TM Centre, gaining a mantra and all that it promised. He looked good. All clean and bright of eye, much was possible for John now.

He stayed with us a while. We all meditated regularly. John had ceased being a junkie, no mean feat as I see it. He put a lot of attention into the TM movement, soon moving away to share with a TM teacher in a very nice house indeed. John was standing up straight, looking beautiful and clear, dressed so well and attending all the meetings.

Before long he was giving the lectures to introduce the concepts TM was based on, to the public. We weren't surprised when he decided to go to Switzerland to do TM teacher training for months on end. We knew that it cost a lot of dollars, and I was surprised to hear that the TM teacher sharing a house with John had paid both their course fees.

Peter was a bit more pragmatic than I was; I still thought these guys walked on water.

"Geoff is gay, mate, and they are lovers." Ah, I thought. It all made sense. In fact, I had already started to wonder if the TM movement was becoming an extension of the local gay scene.

Time passed. We smoked dope sometimes, meditated others, made plans and generally lived. An aeon later, John came to the door in a suit and took us all out to eat. He had been the Maharishi's cook and was home to celebrate and thank us. Nice.

The suit was required dress for TM teachers now, as Maharishi was seeking mainstream credibility. I thought it smelt a bit. Peter thought a long time, and decided out loud that it didn't matter how you marketed it, the technique was still valid.

John was strongly pushing the TM company line that the world must change from the top. The effects would reach the factory floor soon enough if management were all meditative.

Now, I am a working-class boy inside, Peter too; and we flinched a bit at that, as the older TM teacher, Athena, had always marketed TM in a very down-home way.

She had the credibility of being in the first TM teacher-training course ever. Run by Maharishi in India, four people only, and she was the only woman. I hoped she had not taken all this on board. She hadn't; and was soon being severely chastised by the new boys and girls for not behaving properly. This went on for a few weeks and suddenly stopped.

Athena had not changed her ways and the young Turks had been told by the Maharishi to leave her alone and that whatever she decided to do was fine with him. We were very happy and continued to visit her, as it suited our perceptions of the technique better. She gave us coffee and European cakes and listened.

We lived on; sending certain types of TM-interested people to John *et al* and the rest to Athena. John left to be in Sydney and the national headquarters of the TM movement. The house broke up and Peter and I lived in an apartment nearer the city. I bought my first VW van. We all still meditated fairly regularly, saw Athena a bit less, and had a life.

Social contact with the old network of TM found me talking to John years later. Still looking good, he was moving back to town and did I know where he could stay a while? He had a job in a gourmet food shop so he was fine for money.

I lived in the city and had a spare room, so John moved in. Not much stuff, and tidy. We watched TV, John had a special friend who stayed sometimes and other times he went out by himself. All went well.

Peter, John and I, for the sake of Auld Lang Syne, ate together one night and then drank heavily. John, in a fit of camaraderie, began to fill in the gaps. He was prone to get a particular pleasure by upsetting gangs of youth with taunts and running away. The chase was the thing, he said. I noted that he had often known the shortest ways in the city, with comments like "if we hurry – because the stair door shuts at two o'clock".

Peter said he already knew the details as he had been working in a remand centre a while ago and in conversation with a youth over a photo album had been told, "That bastard there in the suit is John the Runner. If I ever catch him, the prick's a dead man." I asked John if he ever was caught. He said sometimes; he got raped as a rule.

I am shaken by all this, but the spirit of the times was tolerance. John had left TM, was moving in guru circles, looking for the centre of some personal cyclone.

We didn't speak of it again until one night he rushed in the door, breathless, flung himself against the wall, and gasped, " Oh God, I hope they didn't see me come in here."

I was terrified, showed no compassion, and explained very clearly that he should not bring this particular pleasure home as it caused me discomfort and that if he did it again I would shove his arse out the letter slot in the door so I would not be disturbed. He felt this was a little strong and moved out a few weeks later.

Again years went by. I was visiting Ross one summer day, cakes and cream in hand, when the door opened and grinning John was there, loving me and making me welcome. He was staying a while and had met Ross through a friend. Small world. He was very pleased, as Ross knew his father and had worked with him for a time.

John knew little of his dad and had spent much of his childhood in boys' homes and with foster parents. These had been hard for him, physically and sexually abusive in the main. He wanted some touch with his father just to get a feel for him. So Ross's knowing was a gift to him. Small world.

He left weeks later after some upsetting incident, and we saw him rarely. John was always moving, finding a different place and after a short while hating it, or someone in it, and moving on excitedly to a new place – only to be again disappointed.

He disappeared for some months, and on his return told Ross a story of being kept, albeit in some comfort, in the bush by a community of hippies, and not allowed to leave because they believed him holy. Ross didn't believe him. I was sure it was true. His presence was always strong and clear with an innocent hope that seemed to be of the beyond. This was why I was always pleased to see him.

Finally we heard he was in India with a new guru, and happily settled. We went on and John faded in memory, appearing only in those conversations about mad bastards we have known.

Without notice as always, he appeared at the door again several years later and asked if he could stay awhile. Of course he could; and to both celebrate and give John a post-India weight gain, we all went to dinner at a local pasta restaurant.

He was moody and upset at the food; the waiters and all that presented itself got a serve of his anger. I was surprised. He had been a bit grumpy and assertive about his situation in the past, but I had never seen him generally abusive. I was sitting next to him, and after the main course he leaned towards me conspiratorially and asked me what I thought of Guru Dev, the TM senior guru, who had taught and chosen the Maharishi to continue the work. I decided to tell the truth.

"Mate, I like the sound of him, but I am always suspicious of the holiness that exists in a wilderness setting. You know, no challenge, not integrated into the world. Like a hot-house rose. I wonder if it would be surviving well out here." I gestured widely with my hands to indicate the world in general.

This was clearly not what John wanted to hear. He decently gave me a chance to redeem myself, saying curtly, "But there were wild animals all silent and peaceful around him. What about that?"

I ploughed on. "Mate, I don't know. It may be true, it may not. I wasn't there and neither was anyone I have ever met. I am still seeing it as a half life. A spirituality in total isolation has less value to me than it once did."

John stood up and at the top of his voice informed me that I had always been patronising and had never liked him at all through the years I had known him. Then, that everybody thought me sanctimonious and that I ought to shut up about holy things or suffer the karmic consequences.

Ross looked interested, so I asked him if I was sanctimonious at all times or not. He looked at me and said, "I think John's a bit crook, mate."

Without any sympathy I turned to John and said, "Why don't you shut up until you have something civil to say?" I went on to tell him he had been rude to everybody for miles and to have a drink and settle down. He walked out of the restaurant and was gone when we got home.

We heard later in the year that he had died the night before in Sydney, at the apartment of a friend. Ross said, "He was too thin, mate. You didn't see them, but when he changed to go out that night he left, he had bruises."

The official cause was pneumonia, but I knew inside that I had a mate who had died of Aids. "Revenge of the rainforest," I said to Ross. He grinned and we had a drink or two.

I told friends. We put a notice in the memorial section of the local paper and in it quoted Leonard Cohen.

*"Even though it's all gone wrong, I stand before the lord of song, with just one word upon my tongue. Hallelujah."*

It was the only one there.

I don't think John would have been afraid to meet his maker. He was as mad as a cut snake, but always hopeful and gently committed.

I miss him.

# NOT QUITE THE PELOPONNESIAN WAR

*"Little circle spin and spin, big wheel turnin'*
*round and around"*
Buffy Saint-Marie

*T*eaching technology at a country high school with the two maddest people I had met in the system for a long time. Dave and Bill were not regular tech teachers.

Two years before, about a month before the event, Bill decided to enter a 24hour pedal prix in a nearby river town with untrained students and no vehicle. We built one, rough but clever, took the kids and placed well. The following year we meant it. Kids trained hard, built a great bike and we were the highest placed public school to finish.

Private schools were a whole different matter: they had masseurs for the riders, houseboat accommodation and chefs with proper hats to feed them. Parental contributions to stand in awe of, they weren't to be beaten by us with the VW Kombi as kitchen and the tent by the track.

Bill was mellow, and worked with fibreglass and all the chemicals. Dave and I were sure he was permanently a bit out of it. Different thinking happened in there. Dave had been a rev-head, building racing boat motors and drinking hard before he came to teaching. He was big. And prone to being blunt regarding administration. The kids loved him. Great engineer. And me. We were an odd lot.

It was Bill's fault really, with his passing remark at the weekly faculty meeting in the pub after work Thursday,

54

"There is a solar challenge across Australia, next year. We could go in it." Dave had drink in and said that was a good idea and let's do it. Like all those ideas, that was the end of it. Except that Bill ordered stuff: materials and solar cells, and contacted a mathematics professor. So we were committed really when they all turned up.

They built a wooden car shape as a mould to make the fibreglass bits, design students organised a frame, elegant bike bits and solar power were placed and a year later there was this wonderful elegant cockroach-shaped vehicle that went like mad.

The kids were extraordinary, country kids, never smoked, shiny cheerful tough boys. Trained by a staff member who had trained Olympic cyclists sometime earlier. We built machines for training and how they suffered. The car was the thing really, Dave was a precise person, so all the made bits were perfect, really perfect. Nothing was less than precise, students made many components which went into the rubbish bins until the standard he wanted was reached.

Bill, as well as being a master of composite materials, was the greatest scammer of sponsorship ever. German companies supplied top-end motors and cogs and chains and we put it together properly. And we sold a million chocolate frogs. The kids got hard. We trained on roads in the bush weekends and worked nights. A trailer was built. Dave painted suitably embarrassing flames on the side, then on the car too. It got named Solar Flare.

To Alice Springs in cars towing convoy and a sort of catering truck I occupied with a team member's mother whose daughter organised team sequences. People from everywhere in the world were there. Some rough cars and some very snappy ones from the US, Asia and Europe. We slept in a sort of barracks and it was hot. Scrutineering happened and we checked out the competition. There was one American, a lovely bloke whose car, Solar Boy, had been ruined by customs. We spent a lot of time helping him put it together again during the evening and after sat late drinking and talking rot. His vehicle looked serious, but Dave felt the build standard was a little shonky. It was too. It got a few hundred metres on day one and broke down.

After days testing various ways of crossing cattle grids without imitating the Titanic, the morning of the start arrived. We left Alice Springs at around 8am at 15-minute intervals. The car looked good, but it didn't seem as fast as we all thought. All cruising, holding our position okay until about 11am, I noticed we were passing all and sundry very quickly. I couldn't figure it, so I asked Dave. "The sun has hit the panels properly mate, we are flying!" Fair enough too. Many panels had been tested and only the most efficient were kept. Some programming trickery was also in play. So we were off. A long way in front at the end of day one with nothing to repair, we ate well and slept well. It happened again the next day.

There is a nice relaxed bit in being a winner, so I got sort of bored just following the car and started listening to the radio transmissions of different teams. Mostly chatter, but reflecting the people and their machine problems, entertaining. The one that was different was the private college. They had purchased the rights to a bike design from the USA and were in all sorts of strife with it. A sort of recumbent cycle with almost vertical front forks, this meant it was easily moved from a straight line travel and really was very unstable. It fell a lot. Enough to give their team a 'special' award from the first aid squad in attendance. The staff were not going to see the machine as faulty, but pushed their riders mercilessly. Encouragement was not evident, more threats of being individually withdrawn and comparisons that were just plain nasty.

We had always been equal in many ways with our drivers, they were always welcome to speak, good-humoured and light. Almost peers, certainly a co-operative team. I was shocked. Abuse was a motivation I had rejected long ago and couldn't believe anybody still did that. But there it was. "You're making a complete dog's breakfast of this, get out and we will put someone in who can ride it properly." Like that. Over and over again. Talk of weakness and even threats of being sent away.

Our drivers were, by contrast, having fun. The machine was remarkable and they pressed on hard. A strange cast and some remarkable moments. One of the boys was the son of an opera singer and was classically trained in the art. His hobby was mountain biking. As he pressed the little car and himself along hour after hour the only sound through the intercom was endless long, slow breathing. He holds the highest speed record for the event still.

Our real competition was from serious racing bicycles and fit adults with token tiny solar panels. A remarkable race for the day's line honours over the last thirty miles between our car and such a bicycle, was won by a very few feet by us. The kids made book on the result and the driver bet on himself. The exhilaration on his face was unbelievable as he was helped from the car. Ruined as he was, his effort was only to hug the Malaysian bike rider and hope that it happened again tomorrow. They were like that all the time.

Not security-minded, we simply parked the car outside wherever we slept and raced it the next morning. This seemed fine, until on the third night, when it was clear to all that this was the car to beat, we woke to shuffling noises near the car at two in the morning. We found a driver from the college pulling wires out of the rear vent of our car. It mattered too much to these people, it was serious business to them. The driver was taken to his team leader and they dealt with it somehow. Whenever the media appeared the college effort was to have the school sign brought out fast and push to interview. It really was business.

The race was days long. We kept quiet and won by hours. Great celebration happened and even then the college was endlessly lauded and praised for its behaviour and sportsmanship. But we won. And then we took the vehicle to the USA and won a world championship with it. Nice and real.

# SWEEPING UP AFTER TM

*What to say, really. Many dear friends, a peer group, reasons, a map, some lovers, lots of dollars gone, and a mess in my head. For all the difficulty, I had a tremendously valuable sequence.*

$\mathcal{F}$or 12 years I did TM, various meditation courses and a number of the Transcendental Meditation's advanced techniques, finally spending the last year practising the TM Siddhis programme.

When I first started it was like a bolt of lightning in the maze, a rational and clear path with great promise at the logical end. As time went on, though, it proved to have some serious shortcomings. They all centred in the same aspect of the technique and were explained as the phenomenon of physiological stress release resulting from the effectiveness of one's meditation.

When any release of accumulated stress, trauma, or fixed patterning begins to occur, the first thing to go is the top bit, the defences. This leaves whatever the reason was for covering it all up, screaming at you like an open wound. This needs to be dealt with, with compassion and humanity. The TM personnel inevitably advised that one was "unstressing" and to meditate and go on with daily life. This was at times extremely difficult. I have not described specifics because they varied from person to person, and in strength, as the process continued.

I watched as from time to time on a weekend course this non-recognition would get too much for an individual; and if they were frightened, angry or in any way negative, they were simply sent away to deal with it alone and unsupported.

I noticed that, when I was working physically, the TM process was more manageable. TM teachers said that this was the integration of the meditation experience with daily life. Aha!

There existed a short yoga sequence approved of by the Maharishi Mahesh Yogi done on the courses. One meditation and one yoga sequence was called a round.

This seems to be recognition that something needed to be added to the technique to aid physiological integration. But rather than integrate this recognition into the public framework of TM, the Maharishi insisted that TM was self-regulating, and would maintain balance, simply by the general activity of daily life. This seemed patently untrue to me, simply because, if it were the case that daily activity integrated the stresses accumulated by daily activity, they would not have accumulated in the first place.

What seemed to be happening was that the TM technique was opening access, through physiology and consciousness change, to deeply rooted physiological stress caused, not by daily life, but by traumatic experience. This left the meditator not only without any mechanism to integrate the release into a conscious comfort zone, but also in the hands of a group that was trained to consider this type of release unacceptable and treated its inevitable appearance harshly.

My own response to this was to begin regular training in a martial art, and to institutionalise an informal arrangement with a friend to be available each for the other during TM rounding courses if we found the internal going was getting tough. This worked well for some time. It lasted until I decided to invest heavily and acquired the TM

Siddhis techniques. This was a whole other thing, much more demanding of both daily time and of lifestyle changes.

Gone was the twenty minutes twice a day and just go on with daily life. A room was set aside. High density foam mattresses covered the floor. Particular clothes were required, so the Siddhi techniques required time to change at each end. The practice took over an hour in the morning and again at night. Certain activities were suddenly deemed inappropriate – alcohol consumption, meat eating... and sex were all thought a little gross for the sensitised physiology.

Mind you, the techniques were effective. The TM Siddhis caused a tremendous opening of the internal aspects of life. This was, as before, not assimilated into the physiology in any TM-approved way other than daily activity. Now, if daily activity was failing to integrate the effects of the simple technique of TM, it seemed unlikely that it would integrate the effects of the TM Siddhis programme.

I began to notice many of my long-term companions becoming more introverted and less comfortable with the world outside the TM group. My own experience was very disquieting. When I realised what was happening, the transition back to the simpler and more or less integratible technique was not quick, easy, or supported by the TM movement.

The effect of the TM Siddhis programme rippled on for a number of years. TM itself proved ineffective in restoring any balance and I began to seek methods that contained physical components, in the hope that they would self-integrate the expansion of consciousness into the physiology inside the practice of the meditation.

A real insight into what the upper echelon of the TM movement became around that time came later when I read Suzanne Segal's *Collision with the Infinite*. The first thirty pages are very clear. The rest of the book goes alright too.

The TM movement has a website in the 21st century. I looked at it recently for the first time, and as a contact point after many years, it was staggering. It seems that Maharishi has long moved beyond the purveying of a simple technique of meditation suitable for all, and has branched into many "subtle sciences". He is, however, discontent with how the world has received him, and has rationalised it by deciding that the current crop of humanity is in its first birth cycle after being animals. His message, he feels, is therefore too subtle for us. If you want to talk about it with him personally, you can do so for a donation of a few million US dollars.

Once, the technique cost a week's pay and a small collection of things for the ceremony. It is only for the wealthy now and, unless a way to integrate it is included, from my perspective they are truly welcome.

Generally speaking, it seems that the cultures that developed meditations were all much older than contemporary western society, and were formed in an environment in every way, except the absolute, different from our own. So it would seem unreasonable to expect that the meditation glove, made for the hand of another, should fit us seamlessly.

I have always found that the meditations of old, not just TM, but other traditional techniques, don't integrate easily in the long term into the structure of our daily life. This, I suspect, is due to the placement of them into niches in the culture they come from. The traditions in India were almost all grown from an individual in isolation, supported by the community.

Even Gautama the Buddha had a major aspect in his teachings of manifest reality as secondary. This may be because it is so nearby and overwhelming of the subtle; but the result in *our* culture looks escapist and socially irresponsible.

I have great admiration for Robert M. Pirsig and his attempts to integrate these apparent opposites. Why indeed would the Godhead be less comfortable on and/or in a motorcycle than in the Himalayas? I can't see any reason.

I see the meditation techniques of these cultures as a critical half of an integrated system that encompasses all aspects of reality. We as westerners have tremendous access to the things of life, and a comfort hitherto unheard of. Any internal discontentment seems therefore not to be easily dissolved with more of the same, but requires an integration of world comfort with the other, that which is beyond the visible.

Traditional methods of meditation are constructed to focus entirely on the unmanifest and this presents difficulties for those of us who need to interface with the world on a daily basis. Inherent in the meditation structure is an initial removal from the world and a refocus on the beyond.

I seek greater integration than this. If these techniques can be either adjusted, or used as a part of an integrated system exclusive of nothing, then their value will be tremendous. Otherwise, I see them as evidence of extremely subtle perception of only part of reality; and not really all that useful in the West.

# WHY BOTHER?

*Why would you try to fix something that was working?*

*I* never took much notice of Matt when we were young. I only take a bit now because gravity took him in our respective middle years to buy the house two doors up from where I live.

He is two years younger than I am. It doesn't matter now, but in my adolescence it rendered him a complete non-event in my life. He never stepped out of line, was okay at school, got a job. 'Mr. Normal'.

I had taken him with me this day because he wanted to buy a present for someone and I thought of Neil's fine woodwork. He bought something from Neil's workshop and we all walked to Max's place for a cup of tea.

For Matt, he had arrived in a part of the world that he had only heard of – at the edge where real old hippies lived. He clearly loved the house and spent the first few minutes looking intensely at all the artefacts arranged therein.

Max made tea and we sat in the big old lounge chairs. Matt said that he really liked the rug. Max told him a short story about the bargaining process involved in its purchase off the street in Rajasthan, then about the customs and airline bribes as he left India, doubling his investment.

Matt said, "I never wanted to go to India. People I knew went, but it didn't interest me." Max replied that he knew a lot of people who weren't keen on India, but that they had all been there.

Matt said to him, "No, not that I didn't like it, I just didn't even think about it."

"Oh – a happy person were you?" asked Max.

I was not sure where this was going to but it seemed a bit narky on Max's part, something I wasn't used to. I looked up from picking the leaves out of my tea. He didn't look pissed off so I waited for Matt to speak.

He was now a bit nervous but said, "Oh yeah, not bad. What do you mean?"

Neil and I knew he didn't have to ask, but Matt was new in town. Max breathed in and started. "Why, in God's name, would anybody with an ounce of contentment go to India to get sick, risk life and limb, take bad drugs, get ripped off, get thin, and come home completely fucked in the body department? Well?"

He looked around like a teacher in a classroom. I took a punt.

"Enlightenment, man. Our culture doesn't even countenance the idea of the impersonal beyond, let alone have mechanisms to let you chase it."

Max replied immediately. "Well, I reckon that that's not the tree, that's the flower. It looks to me more that you wouldn't go to another culture as foreign as India just for its cultural jewellery. I reckon that to even accept the existence of enlightenment as a westerner, you need to be fairly pissed off with your own culture's benefits."

I thought about the Sixties – and it was definitely a time of disenfranchisement. The cultural change of the day was rapid beyond previous experience and the cultural mechanisms of our parents, who came from simpler times, fell over immediately. Leaving us – well, *me* anyway – with no cultural base that I trusted.

Shit, a society that had something as ugly as the Vietnam War going and showed it to us in our lounge rooms, must be totally fucked. I wanted bugger all to do with it, rejected it with religious fervour and looked to everything that wasn't mainstream culture as though it might just have the Holy Grail in it somewhere.

But there was something that wasn't being noticed so I said, "Not only that stuff! Some of us who weren't cultural lost souls did this trip."

Max screwed his eyebrows together, then lifted one and said, "Who?"

I answered him in my clever dick voice. "I know one nice middle-class boy who did the fashionable thing and gobbed 500 microgrammes of pure Sandoz acid one Saturday night and spoke of unity the next day and for some time thereafter. *He* went."

Max, who spent his days sorting the inconsistencies of his experience into his thinking, was clearly impressed by this. Acid could expose the beauteous innards of oneself, particularly in its pure form; regardless of the place you fitted in society before you took it.

I felt good and so I went on. "He was not completely understood by his friends, who reckoned he was mad. He started to look for some place to be that recognised the thing that he had been to. I liked him; he knew and he ached. All he wanted to do was go home."

"Mike Houghton," said Max.

"Yeah... right!" I was not surprised that Max knew Mike, who was out there for a couple of years in the mid-Sixties, finding eventually that the Buddhist ethos was one he could be in with some reality. He is now called Abhinyarno, which means something very nice, and is a Rinpoche monk in some tropical Asian mountain range.

Matt is looking a little confused at this point, but as I turn to him with summary in mind, he asks me, "Do you two always talk like this?"

I thought Neil would fall out of his chair from laughing so hard. We all watched him for a few moments – he had tears in his eyes, he was so deeply affected.

He pushed himself up a bit and said to Matt, "Every time I've seen them together for years, a major event in world conversation happens. They don't fit anywhere properly anymore, so there is a deep need to touch the elephants' graveyard we come from. I'm okay just listening – they will cover all the ground if you wait."

Matt nodded slowly for just a bit too long. He looked from me to Max and back again; then asked, "So hippies were made from people who don't get on in their culture, or were given a nudge with LSD?"

I thought that a bit simplistic, but not wrong.

"Sounds OK," I said, but I wasn't really comfortable.

"Not just lazy bastards looking for an easy time?"

Oh, fuck! *That's* a hard one. There's a lot going on in there. I looked at him. He really did want to know. He was taking a new look at the standard responses out of where he comes from, so the question was a bit deeper than it seemed.

Neil spoke. This is not all that common, so I was attentive. He was the best one to talk to Matt at this point, because he had the credibility of being a successful craftsman and so was not defending his laziness.

"It wasn't an easy time, Matt. And lazy people couldn't do it. If you were looking for a soft option, then denying your culture and pushing yourself to post-intellectualism with fine chemicals and foreign concepts was not the way to go. I always admired surfers as a nice civil way to drop out. Quick and Zenny."

Matt looked around. Neil had opened up completely new ground for him. Judging by the look on his face, he was doing a bit of reassessment of stuff way down there where you live.

I was surprised when he turned to me and said, "I used

to call you Shirley way back then because of your hair; I'm a bit sorry now."

I looked at him. I'm not too easy with sudden male bonding, but managed to pat his shoulder and say, "That's alright, mate – I wasn't listening to you anyway."

We laughed; and were just at the part where you don't know what to do next, when Max got up, patted his belly and said to us all as if it were truly important, "Do you want more tea?"

We all did. I picked out the tea-leaves again.

" Listen, man," I said to Max, "I'm going to get you a fucking tea strainer for Christmas."

"I already have one," he replied, pointing towards the kitchen.

"Ah."

# ROSS MEETS RABINDRANATH

*I suffer.*

 oss is sweating, on a plane to Singapore. Otherwise all is very good indeed. He looks tense as well, so I ask. "Na, I am all good, Gimpy. It's just a pain in my guts. It will go." In Singapore it went. So we shopped and slept then caught the plane to India.

Again the pain. No complaint, so I ignore it all and we settle into Bombay and then Pune. After a day buying the stuff for our small apartment we sleep. I wake to groaning and run to find Ross on his mattress in a ball. Pale and grimacing. "Get a doctor Gimps. I am fucking dying here."

I ran downstairs, and miraculously found our almost personal rickshaw driver who had adopted us only the day before. He knew where the doctor was and drove stupidly fast all the way. It took a while to sort the way through surgery administration; the doctor tidied things and came to see Ross. We walked into the apartment and the mattress was empty. We looked on the balcony, Ross was there, pale and shaking, trying to stand up by pulling himself with the wall. The doctor, a very nice young man with an early balding issue, saw him and immediately began to chide me for not explaining how serious it was. I had mildly abused his staff to get his attention so I wondered what he was used to.

Then, after some pressing and screaming, he announced his suspicion of kidney stones. "Very painful, sir," he informed Ross, who replied in Australian that he had worked that out himself before the good doctor's arrival. I was used as if a translator from this point.

We were to go to a written address and have an ultrasound to confirm the diagnosis and after that return to him for action. Some painkillers were given. No prescription necessary it seemed. Gimpy took some and we left. In the rickshaw and heading into a very odd part of town, the driver said, "Don't worry, sir, you will certainly be safe," as we got out. He was keen to leave and required quite a lot of money not to.

The address was nearby and I helped Ross to stagger into the surgery door. We were the only westerners inside and receiving the attention that deserved. The receptionist was a little uninterested until Ross folded downwards onto the floor without a sound. Then she dashed into the doctor's rooms speaking loudly in Hindi.

We were taken straight in. There was an elderly woman on the examination table so nobody knew what to do until the doctor shooed her off and waved her out. Ross was in trouble, but he didn't like that and let the doctor know. "I will see her next, sir, now come," as he motioned to the table. "Still warm," grimaced Ross. "Nice."

The Doctor listened to my story, read my little paper from the other Doctor and proudly told me that I was definitely at the right place, as his equipment was the most modern possible. "Very expensive, sir, the latest from Germany." The information was clearly to explain to me the monumental numbers that were later to appear on the account, I was sure. I looked at what was clearly an ancient ultrasound machine with utter dismay. It could easily have been from the English occupation and salvaged from their army as they left. The screen, as it rested and waited to display Ross's interiority, was the size of a shirt pocket and covered with interference, while the rest deeply resembled an old jukebox.

Ross was gelled and examined, wincing whenever touched by the sensor. The screen was discussed and the doctor made a phone call. From the moving snow on the tiny screen he had found 'appendicitis' and had referred us to a doctor at the new hospital in Koregaon Park.

Ross dressed, I paid enough rupees to allow the doctor to surely buy at least one new machine, and we took our rickshaw to the 'Ruby Hall' Hospital. This was better, close to Osho Ashram, and to where we were living. People helped us in and asked for money after. Ross was given an appointment and we waited. Everybody waited. And nobody seemed to be called in anywhere. Ever. Asking the reception desk, as Ross was seriously pale and wan at this stage, it came to light that the doctor was late and when he arrived the appointments would begin.

He arrived three hours after we were seated. I was hopeful, and rightly so, as we went first. "To ensure that all was proper," the new Doctor prodded Ross deeply and painfully, read the ultrasound thief's note, gave Ross a needle, Ross slept. Nice.

"I will be removing the appendix at six o'clock tomorrow morning. It is very serious, and you will need to bring these drugs." He wrote a list. Whew.

I went to use the toilet, got lost and finally returned to find Ross gone. Nobody wanted to help me find him, and at last the young woman who was washing the floor over and over again came and said she had cleaned a room and my friend was in it. She showed me and, as it proved true, I was grateful and paid her. Ross had a drip in his arm and was still asleep.

I set up a bed in the little annex room provided for relatives to stay in, organised food to be delivered and waited. And waited some more. A nurse came and adjusted the drip after some time, and said, "Your friend will wake up soon." He did. He had told the doctor the toilet was too dirty for him to be ill in and was given another injection. I had managed to use it, but got the point. He remembered coming into a lift in a wheelchair and now this.

I still had the list of drugs to purchase from the drug shop downstairs and did so, "4000 rupees only, sir." I am gonna let him die next time; I told him this and he confided that his effort at the wall was not to stand but to jump off. He is tough, so I realised it was time to commit. I explained that he was to have his appendix removed in the morning, he sat up in bed, said "Pigs fucking ring I am.", and pulled out his drip. I gathered up my stuff and caught up with him at the elevator. I made him wait while I sold back the drugs at a reduced price, and we caught a rickshaw home.

The next day we went to the local ayurvedic bloke and he voted for the kidney stones then gave Ross what seemed to be a bottle of sherry in the hope of passing them. He liked it and took me to dinner the next night, nice. We sat and ordered, Ross drank gulps of medicine regularly and became very humorous with the waiter.

As we ate, he took my handwritten book of poems and jottings from my bag. He began to read them I noticed his shoulders begin to heave ever so gently. Sobs started. I warned him, but it was hopeless. Slowly he began to weep, and slid gently to the floor with the book in his hand, sobbing loudly. People were astonished. I pretended equanimity and continued to eat. That was working fine until the waiter came and asked Ross if he was okay. Pointing at the book Ross sobbed at the poor man, "It is too beautiful, (*gasp*) too beautiful! This man, (*points at me*) is surely the reincarnation of Rabindranath!" He sobbed harder and refused to get up. "I can't, mate, this is wonderful, so wonderful"

From time to time he looked at the book and began to wail and sob loudly. I paid the bill and left. He followed me instantly and gave the book back. I was shaking my head and about to tell him of his true nature, when he grinned hugely and said, "Come on, Gimpy, don't be a sook. You have been serious as a priest for bloody days."

# WALLY GETS BUSTED

*I suspect the world has always been a strangely twisted place
and that the function of society is to contain the Pythonesque
nature of things under cover so that we all don't piss
ourselves laughing.*

This year is good. I can afford a nice holiday. Not to India this time, but to Byron Bay, staying with Peter and Maree. Peter is taking time off and we are cruising about eating beach lunches, elegant breakfasts, drinking wine; and today, visiting our old mate Wally.

Wally lives in an arrangement of hydro-electrified vehicles in the back of Nimbin. When more people come to stay he gets more old buses to suit.

The opposite also applies.

Not for us today the 3 kilometre walk after the track finishes. Wally is in a nearby town at his sister's place for a holiday and to see his visiting mum. A nice little split-in-half wooden place, near the beach. Lots of palms and tropical growth out front. We know Wally is there, as his recently acquired big old station wagon is parked across the drive.

I haven't known Wal as long or as well as Peter but I am always pleased to see him.

He is an archetypal old hippie activist, was highly placed in Social Security in the early Sixties and is still well informed in the mechanisms of the department. He goes in to bat for the nice old hippie mums whose entitlements are not coming to them and is involved in some way in the

Nimbin Chamber of Commerce. I have difficulty imagining their meetings as a group of august business types, but who knows? Then there is the Community Centre that he helped create. The list goes on.

At the door, some young girl I don't recognise answers, and Peter asks for Wally. She disappears, he comes back. I haven't seen him for a few years. His dreads are huge. And grey.

"Hey, man. How are you?"

Peter answers that he is fine, and we all hug. Wal is very thin. He turns to me, says I look good. I say I feel good, man. His eyes – I had forgotten. Blue, piercing and clear. Wally is sharp. We go in.

The inside surprises me. I am expecting it to be like the outside, tropical, elegant and simple. Not so.

We sit on old, beat-up club lounge chairs. There is a Laminex table, not-new cups, and all sorts of clutter. All is clean, and a bit crowded. The girl turns out to be Wal's daughter, who excuses herself to meet a friend and go to the beach. Wally's mother is sitting at the table. Peter knows her and chats about her health. I am introduced to her and we bond.

She gets a cup of tea for everyone. All the cups are different sizes and shapes. I wonder how she chooses. More chat. Wally needs a fag and we go out.

Wally smokes 30 Viscounts a day. He will surely die soon; he has two of them in his hand now. We break them open and roll a joint. Hmmm – big.

Smoking, smoking.

"When did you get the car, man?" I like to talk about cars.

"About three weeks ago, it goes real quick. I love it." Wally tells us the price, the guy he bought it from, and the boys at the service station admiration story.

We sit. The joint is small now and I get paranoid about the smell and turn to Wally. "Will we get busted here, man?"

"More likely thousands of neighbours and their friends will turn up any minute to suck on it." I believe him. We suck hard and finish it quickly.

Sitting.

Time passes.

Wally says, " I got busted once."

Later on, Peter replies. "I remember."

I have no idea and, desperate to know, ask. Peter gets comfortable and Wally starts.

"It was the year I was staying at Jo and Craig's place." Wally stops.

I am terrified he is going to go all intellectual about what year it might have been so say, "Oh, yeah," like it makes sense to me.

Wal settles, and goes on. "They were at the end of that beautiful road in the hills – God, that was lovely. So, I am walking down there slowly and grocking the scenery..."

Grocking! Wow! *There* is a word from the depths. I feel good.

" ...Anyway, these cops in a car go past, slow down and check me out. I smile and wave and they drive straight on up the road. It was a dead end so I knew they would be back." Wally is grinning. "They *did* come, then stopped and asked where I was going. 'Home, man.' I probably shouldn't have said man, but as it turned out, they would have stopped and searched me anyway.

"I turned out my pockets. They made me turn all the linings inside out. Very friendly and just like policemen they were. I started to empty my bag out and the big one just took it and tipped it onto the bonnet of the car. Lots of empty fag packets – I don't like to litter, you know." I nod. Peter is sitting silently, apparently attentive, but I suspect he is somewhere else altogether.

I have lost track. "Dope is stronger than it used to be, eh?"

I say in the distance, to anyone. Peter says, "Yep. Hydroponics"

Wally has his mind in gear and explains. "It would be the most fucked around with plant ever, man. Years of cloning and pollination with all the breeds, colchisine, breeding to eight times the strength and smelling bad. No wonder I can't remember what I was talking about. Fuck!"

I thought about this for a while; and suddenly Wally went on talking.

"Anyway, there was a single paper spliff in the bag. It rolled off the car onto the ground. The big cop picked it up and asked me what it was. I told him. Busted! In the car being taken home for the big search. I knew Jo would be there. She would be cool, and we hadn't had dope for a while, so I was confident."

I thought of Jo, tall and strikingly pretty. Cops would like her.

"We knocked at the door and Jo answered. I still don't know why I didn't use my key. She got their attention and cool as a cucumber, said, 'Come in, look around if you like.' They tore the place apart. Kept finding little stashes of dope. Jo was following them, saying, 'Oh, there that is. Wow, I was wondering where that went.'

"She made them tea in matching cups and they told her how dangerous drugs were. She listened very carefully and got a warning. They took her dope too. I had about a tenth the quantity and got summonsed."

Peter looks up and says, "Crappy legs, mate, that'll be what that is."

I can't believe it. He must be as whacked as I am and still he makes a coherent comment. I am so far out of it I had forgotten he was there, and now Wally answers as well. These are tough old men.

"I reckon they are all right. Anyway, I was really pissed off because the copper who had searched me was really nice.

Gave me advice on how not to get busted again."

Peter and I look up, waiting. Wally says, "He had done a course, and the key thing, according to police educators, was that the difference between followers of fashion and hippies was simple. Hippies carried a bag."

I don't believe it.

Wally goes on. "So, son, he said to me, get rid of the dilly bag and you won't see us again."

Wally looks completely flummoxed. Peter is off his chair, absolutely folded with laughter. I am worried about him, so I say to Wally, "Did you make that up?"

He says, "No, man; it's true."

No hope for Peter, we leave him in hysterics and walk to Wal's new car. I say, "Shit, I bet *this* goes! It's the big V8."

Wal is a total blank. I explain. He says, "I didn't look under the bonnet when I bought it. That'll be why it uses heaps of petrol."

I suddenly realise that none of us share a planet with the others, sit, and join Peter in hysteria.

# WE DON'T GET BUSTED

*"Don't touch my bags if you please, Mr. Custom's man."*
                                                    Arlo Guthrie

*P*eter and I lived close to the city suburb. It was 1969, a place to spend our summer of love. Childers Street it was called. Forever in our legends as though we lived in the whole street, it was a small porch frontage, only busy because there was a theatre nearby.

Peter and I were the nice young hippies, all flowing hair and right clothing. Robbie, a mate from the country town I lived in, was in the front bedroom, an apprentice mechanic, and not with the house programme at all really. He was trying to build a different kind of life.

Peter and I were working. He was the paymaster at some brick-making place, and I was doing machinery maintenance at an orange juice factory. At night we sat after brown rice, smoked or drank, and made philosophy happen.

The drug squad, headed locally by a Scotsman of legendary nastiness, had busted someone where I worked. One of his favourite and less brutal tricks was to deal leniency for names.

Peter knew. When I introduced the bust and the stories of Jock as after dinner chatter he said, "We'll be next. The poor bastard will have given your name."

I doubted it, but we cleaned up anyway. You know, shifted the weed, not actually cleaned up. We would have been a bad catch; small-time smokers, and opportunists really, more committed to meditation than the hooch. Still, we cleaned up.

Some time later, the cleaning-up resolve long past, and during another evening after dinner while Peter and Robbie were out somewhere, I was reading in the lounge. A visiting stayer called Chris Rick was sitting opposite and there was a knock on the door.

One piece of our local mythology was, after answering the door, to come back inside to all assembled and announce that it was the drug squad. Jolly remarks always followed. This time it *was* the drug squad. There was a suit waving a search warrant and three shadowy grumps behind.

I went inside and told Chris that the drug squad had come. He stood up and cheerfully announced that he would make a pot of nice tea for them, and without missing a beat, very coolly did so as they marched into the lounge in single file.

Chris knew how this all worked and said that he wanted to be present as the search progressed, and that one of us should be witnessing the progress as it happened. So I found myself alone with two large DS officers in the back room where I slept. It had once been some sort of kitchen and had a small wood stove in one corner that I used as a shelf.

I was terrified and the big boys knew it. It suited their purpose so they leaned on me with questions about what I was doing. I shocked them by both being employed *and* having no idea of the surname of the person making the tea, even though he had lived there a while.

I painted a picture of a country boy recently moved and not fully understanding the ways of the big city. All was going well until the black spoon in the cup on the stove was noticed. Yoghurt of several days ago I insisted. They carefully packaged it for analysis. I began to feel confident. We might all survive this. After they had inverted my mattress, left my bedding ruined on the floor and emptied all my stuff onto the bed remnants, my pair moved to the kitchen.

I could see they were troubled. We had not yet evolved to the higher order sort of hippie that has tidiness and cleans. Dirty dishes, empty bottles all about and Robbie's rifle lay disassembled on the table. An air rifle we had that day used to blow many colours of paint on the kitchen cupboard stood dripping and slowly setting in the corner.

I decided to charade the need for a drink to calm my simple country nerves. Permission granted from the lawmen, I started. Finding the bottle of whisky was easy; a glass to drink from was too hard. Chris had used the last cups for the tea, some of which had been drunk while my room was being torn up. In the sink glasses would be, with every filthy dish we had. Even if I found one, there was no way to turn on the tap to clean it as I would then need to shift dishes most foul to find the tap itself. I gave up and drank from the bottle.

A bad moment to do so really, as the bigger of my two reached into an overgrowing cardboard box of greenery on the floor and toyed with the dirt beneath, and asked me what this was.

Barely managing to not spit whisky or laugh, I said, "Oh, that's the cat's shit, box mate. He doesn't use it much, the back door is always open."

His response was difficult to describe or believe. He sternly picked it up, and the urine-wet bottom of the box collapsed, releasing all the dirt and undergrowth to the floor. His mate took a plastic garbage bag from a kit they had left by the door and they put handfuls of the cat box and its month-deep growth into the proffered bag, folded it and put it away for later analysis.

I knew we had no dope and so was feeling quite relaxed, like I was at the theatre.

"What next?" I asked.

"The two front rooms. One of you in each, please."

The kitchen had not been searched, so I asked if they wanted to do that first. The big guy sternly directed me into the front room without saying please this time. Chris and the other two went to the second room, every surface painted with navy blue flat paint that stole the light as you shone it. Peter's stuff was in there. Nice and tidy. I could hear the searchers making comments about the décor as we went into Robbie's room.

I went first and said, "This is not my space, guys. It belongs to someone who's not here."

I wondered where they were. Back soon I hoped.

Big said, "God, what a bloody pigsty."

I couldn't see the problem – what they were used to, searching hovels and harassing people – that this was having such an effect. I looked around. Robbie was not at ease with himself inside and the radio was on as always. A big old 1950's radiogram, lights on and going loud. He slept with a loaded shotgun next to the bed and would dive to grab it if woken.

A favourite trick in early times, before we realised how real the problem was, was to get someone to stand on the gun, then all lean over and look directly at him sleeping, turn the radio off suddenly and all hum loudly. God, he would grab the gun, scream obscenities and threaten to kill us all, but not before we had seen the look of terror pass over his face. So we stopped.

I pointed the gun out to the officers and said that it was without doubt loaded and the safety, if it existed, would be off. They nodded. I think they were grateful.

I looked around again. The bed had been slept in for weeks and never made, messy. There were piles of clothes on the floor, and in one corner on a set of unfolded clean sheets, courtesy of his mother, were the internals of the motor of Rob's car, all lined up, clean and shiny. The room was dark and lit only by the radio dial, as the light had failed some time ago. It looked a bit squalid, but I didn't see a pigsty.

The smaller officer made his way across the room and began to go through the clothes pile near the corner. He had a powerful torch and was checking everything. To be there at all, he had to straddle another pile of clothes and bend forward. Suddenly in mid-sort, he stood, jumped back, and shrieked, "Shit! What the fuck is that?" pointing at the recently straddled pile of clothing.

I saw it move. His mate, Big, had his hand on his shoulder-holstered gun. I said, "Oh come on, guys. Settle down."

I leaned over and picked up the clothes pile. I honestly didn't know what to expect and was relieved to find the cat underneath in a pizza box, chewing at the remains of some vintage pizza crusts. He did look a bit demented. I didn't blame him really. He had come to us from real strong physical abuse and we had calmed him deeply by shotgunning him with a paper bag filled with therapeutic dope smoke. A couple of days of this and he was a mellow sort of lunatic, happily resident under things, peeping out. Later he went to the country and lived well in a shearing shed full of mice until he expired of old age and fatness.

As I picked him up by the scruff of the neck I heard the door open and in came Peter and Rob, a bit drunk.

"What are you doing with the lizard, man?"

It was Peter. The cat's name was Plastic Lizard the Third, and the lizard was his short form for informal discussion.

Of course I replied, "The drug squad is here, man, and he was disturbing them; so I am going to take him out the back and drown him."

"Better make them some tea then."

"No need, Chris already did."

Up until this moment it had occurred to neither of them that the drug squad really was there, but as the suits appeared they saw the truth.

"What the fuck are you bastards doing in my room?" Rob demanded of the nearest officer, my mate Big, the one with gun-drawing tendencies.

"Turn around and place your hands on the wall, please ,son." Robbie turned and placed his hands in the position. I knew this would not go well.

Peter was nearly finished being frisked by one of Chris's coppers. One each now, I thought.

Now Robbie was a bit rough. His jeans had no pockets; that is, the cotton liners were long gone, and he wouldn't let any of our visiting girlfriends sew braid over the holes they left. As Big put his hand in Rob's pocket, it came to light that the week's ration of underwear had been used and what the poor copper found was Rob's ample member in his hand.

"Are you a fucking poofter, mate? We are engaged now, you know, and if you don't like it, get your fucking hands off my dick!"

That was when the coppers decided we didn't fit the pro-file of whatever they were looking for. Two of them took Rob aside into his room for a quiet word and Chris's two took a quick look around the back yard then gathered their kit, the yoghurt spoon, the bag of catshit and left with the first pair, who had by then finished with Rob.

As he left, Big turned to me and said, "You should get out of here and tidy yourself up, son. I bet your parents would be ashamed." He turned to Rob and told him to watch his mouth in future or there would be trouble. Rob invited him to return alone and hear what he had to say then.

Chris closed the door, and Peter said, "That went well. Lucky they didn't find the stash under the garbage bin out the back." Just to be on the safe side we stayed up late and smoked it.

# I TAKE A BEATING

*Have you ever truly been a stranger in a strange land?*
*It's not good.*

"*Y*ou have *got* to be joking, mate! I don't see *you* as a soldier."

I have idly mentioned spending 18 months in the Army as a regular soldier while much younger.

"And you joined up? God, not even National Service! What the fuck possessed you to do that?"

Neil doesn't swear as a matter of course, so I know he is astonished. His voice gives it away too, all a bit up high and fast. I rarely mention my service to my country. It had that nasty, short and brutal flavour to it. Best forgotten I think. A long time ago too.

I drink tea, hoping the conversation will turn to something gentler. Sadly not to be, as Max, who has known me forever, says, "He needed someone to drink with I think."

Jesus, *that's* close to the mark. I wanted a strong peer group in my late adolescence, and in desperation I found the familial promise of the respected and instantly recognisable Army very attractive to try for a place in the world.

Max is not stopping. He goes on with the same accuracy as before.

"I remember that time. You were absolutely non-fitting. Your parents had not functioned well, the job in Telecom was finished, nowhere to stay at length, and you owned nothing. It was one thing or the other and you spun out, man, trying to find a nice new family to replace the fucked-up one."

"I did, Max."

Attention comes, as I rarely call anyone by name. "And I paid; it was the worst of times indeed."

Neil, ever the therapist and curious as well, says, "Well tell us about it. It will do you good I am sure and it's about time we had the dirt on you."

I begin at the worst time. This will mean no more Army stories, as they will not want to hear more mean shit and that will suit me fine.

"Look, you two know. I was always a bit hippie-minded and that's okay most places, but not there. The Army doesn't want people in a mellow state. It doesn't suit their purposes. The whole system is set up to keep you a bit twitchy. Happy people do not make good soldiers."

Nods come. I go on.

"They can tell, you know. If you're the wrong material, they smell you like a rat. Then you are a sort of pressure release valve for everybody. It doesn't matter what happens to you if you are not one of the group. I was innocent and clean compared to the boys who came on the bus with me. All streetwise, blooded and fight-minded. I honestly thought that I would be joining a band of noble warriors. The truth was a bit bloody hard to take."

I notice new tea has arrived steamy hot and, as I sip, I find more honey than usual. I am amongst lovers here. Nice to be reminded.

"Ah, shit. It was horrible – the whole thing. It could go wrong on you very seriously in a moment.

"One day, not long before a public guard duty – very important and inspiring to the boys it all was – we were learning new rifle drills. It was midsummer and 110 degrees. After a couple of hours I was fucked. I needed water and a nice lie down. It is close to the end and as a parting sort of joke, the Sergeant wonders in a cynical voice if anyone wants anything made clearer? Then we could do a little more practice on it perhaps.

"I can't believe it. Oakley, a thick bastard and rough as guts, is asking for more. A lot of us, including me, tell him to fuck off. I am behind him and he focuses on me. I'm the whipping boy, right? He says he will fix me up as he should have before and that I was a useless bastard that needed putting down long before this. We do more drill."

I sip again.

"A few minutes after, I am walking inside the hallway outside our rooms and am king-hit from behind. Oakley and his mates bustle me into an empty room and he is in front of me. The others let go of me. I am no real threat to Oakley as he is huge. He hits me all over for a long time. I can't defend myself properly. His mates bump me around.

"So I take it. I have been hit before – fully trained by my mad mother to separate from this kind of stuff until it passes. I watch myself losing consciousness; fall down. Oakley picks me up by the hair and smashes a front tooth with his fist. My mouth fills with blood. Suddenly it's over. Someone has come in and is talking to him, saying it is enough. I am hustled up the hallway into the showers. All the way people are looking at me and saying "Jesus-fucking-Christ". I am imagining such a mess. I see in the mirror that it's true. I shower. People come and go."

Neil is regretting asking, I see. More tea is slurped and I go on.

"So I get dressed, and eat. That night the Sergeant asks what happened to my face. He knows of course. I tell him I slipped in the shower and then bumped into the door. I am not believed so I repeat it. Again I am taken into the empty room – this time with only Sergeant Carter. He talks.

"It comes to light that he wants Oakley out and I can help. Now I am looking at a transfer to another platoon and

RIKTAM BARRY

some credibility with the powerful and I am not having any of it."

"Scared of more beating?" Neil asks. He does not like this much.

"No. I was pissed off. Where were these people during the weeks of crap I was getting? Giving me more. Freedom in a lie, mate. I told him I slipped in the shower and bumped into the door. He said he knew Oakley had hooked into me and I better tell the truth or he would frog-march me down to spend the night in the clink.

"Now *that* made me shit myself. All kind of stories from the unregulated jail – all out of sight in there, mate. People came back seriously humbled. I went for it anyway. I told him again I had slipped in the shower and bumped into the door. He went out and called a heads in the hall assembly. Doors opened along the corridor and everybody stood, waiting.

"Sergeant Carter took me out and said to all and sundry that I was a useless prick and without doubt the Army would be better off without me, but that I had more guts in my little finger than most of the arseholes present, 'especially *you*, Oakley, you pus-filled bag of shit'.

"What he didn't like and went on to say publicly and loudly, was that Oakley had taken his mates in to help and had king-hit me first. Bad behaviour from a soldier. Beatings must be given honourably and taken the same way. Now *I* was the hero, Oakley the bastard. I was clearly in a madhouse.

"It was like that all the bloody time. Dissonant with reality, all like a black comedy. Once I was clearing up an office and found papers on the function of all kinds of Army stuff. Drill, for instance, was to instil an instinctive obedience to command in the soldier. Tension was to be maintained as it enabled the soldier to function more appropriately in combat situations – all shit like that.

88

"I am sick of this and I want new tea. You want to hear more?"

Max got up.

"I'll get a bottle of wine, we'll get shitfaced, and that'll be better."

# AUSTRALIAN INVOLVEMENT IN
# THE VIETNAM WAR

*The Australian Army, probably any army, is held together*
*by a collective agreement to a lot of rules. About who is in*
*charge and who is not, who gets hit and who doesn't. They all*
*agree to dress the same and operate on a bunch of pre-decided*
*cues for all the values of their little society. The cost is high.*
*Humour has little place. No sense of lightness remains.*
*All regards power and control.*

*C*hosen forms like this have no basis in reality and from time to time the veneer of the military disappears, leaving human beings.

I had two main companions when I was in the Army. One Private Clewes and one Private Zaffino. 'Clewesy' and 'Zeke', respectively. Clewesy was small and a bit hairy, curly, head-covering hair, and always his face signalled the need for a shave. Zeke was big. Tall and muscular, big shoulders from the throwing of boxes of stuff about in his parents' fruit shop.

Added to the Army effort to keep us fit, Zeke was a force. Once, he was accosted in our local hotel, the Rooty Hill pub, by a large man of particular belligerence. Zeke fought hard, felt no pain and suddenly concluded the matter by picking the bloke up and hurling him through the glass portion of the door. He landed heavily down the steps and found himself with a broken leg. Zeke explained that people weren't that much heavier than a couple of bags of potatoes.

A week later, Clewesy and I were having a quiet one and this same bloke on crutches was saying that he would have done fine if the bastard hadn't broken his leg. Clewesy and I didn't fight people; we drank a bit and looked to have fun.

Zeke was a bit older than we were and, after annoying enough people in the system, he was posted to Vietnam for active duty. We were not infantrymen; we were Air Dispatchers, droppers of supplies, with parachute attached, from planes to proper soldiers below. They referred to us as 'parcel-pushing, pistol-packing poofters'. (Pistols because you can't carry a rifle in a plane.) So Zeke was in no danger really – only one parcel-pushing poofter died in Vietnam, a bloke called 'Ocker'. His name was Ockmazich and he was stabbed in a bar fight. I knew him and wasn't surprised.

We were dramatic young men, however, and a comrade-in-arms deserved to be sent off properly. As Zeke was a bit worried, we planned to part company in the Australian manner – he would leave comatose from drink.

He was due to leave at 6:00am from the guard room where he would sleep, as his personal room contents had been handed back to the store. We thought that, starting sometime the day before, we would dress him in expendable clothes and feed him drink, arriving back at 5:30 am to dress him in his jungle killer gear and pour him into a truck. A simple plan – not much to go wrong really.

It started well. Clewesy took his car into inner Sydney and parked it where we were to leave the train. He then caught the train back. We met him at the station. Rooty Hill is a long way out in the western suburbs; we took a commuter train into Central Station, stopping at each station on the way for a beer. We were all over the place as we headed for Kings Cross in Clewesy's retrieved car, a sort of tough English thing, large and comfortable. I feel sure it was late afternoon, as the sun was shining.

The sequence of events becomes blurred at this point.; I seem to have been semi-conscious until about 2:00am the next morning, but I am sure the following things happened.

We were at a strip club, seated in the front row, and popping the corks of cheap bubbly wine at strippers as they come past us. We were asked to leave and didn't like it. There was an abuse exchange outside the club until Zeke grabbed the tout by the front and picked him up. Several big guys flicked themselves off the wall, no longer laughing, their right hands coming from their pockets to reveal brass-knuckled fists. I pointed this out to Zeke, who threw the tout at them as we ran.

We took Zeke to a nice prostitute who, after a long time, came to the door, angrily saying that we should get him out of there, as the prick had gone to sleep on top of her. I explained that he was a bastard to everyone and that it was not personal and gave her more money.

We yelled at policemen and swam naked somewhere; then at about 1:30am Zeke said, "I want to say goodbye to my mum."

His mother was asleep somewhere in a suburb called Blacktown, where they ran the fruit shop. As it was very close to Rooty Hill we tried to deter him with the promise of good times, but he was a good son and was having none of it.

We bought a bottle of Scotch and started to drive, arriving miraculously – given Zeke's directions – at around 2:30am. A nice house for a moment as we drove up, then turned off the car lights – to find no streetlights were shining. We stumbled with Zeke to his front door, where he bashed and yelled.

"I didn't know you spoke Italian, mate," I said. He spelled his surname and slurred at me, "What fucking language do you reckon I speak? Wake up, dickhead!" A light came on and some time later the door opened, to reveal a nice-looking middle-aged Italian woman. I began to apologise, but Zeke started to cry, drunkenly fucking Vietnam loudly and sniffling "I'm going to die".

His mother turned and, with us all following her, went straight to the kitchen. Good strong coffee and sweet cakes came. We talked. I liked her, an unsung hero type of mother. Zeke slept in his chair, head on the table, sitting suddenly up from time to time to either curse Asians as fucking slopes or cry that he was going to die.

Clewesy and I ignored him and made conversation with Mrs. Zaffino, apologizing and thanking. We had drunk little Scotch as Zeke had been a bit greedy. Clewesy and I were sobering – and tired.

Suddenly vertical and his chair fallen, Zeke proclaimed, "I need a piss." As he spoke he reached for the front of his trousers and then turned toward the front door and left us. "Glad he went outside really," I said. "I was a bit frightened there for a minute."

His mother lowered her head a bit and smiled, and Clewesy laughed. We sat for a long, long time. I finished another coffee. We had cake again, and finally Clewesy thought we had better look for Zeke. So we left, promising Mrs. Zaffino that if we found him we would take him somewhere else.

We looked about the front and back yards without success. Into the car and we drove slowly around the block, then expanded driving circles, stopping and shouting from time to time – all fruitless. As there was bush on both sides of the road that Zeke could easily have disappeared into, we decided to leave him and go. I was relieved.

We turned left, over a slight rise in the gravel road, and as Clewesy accelerated away, the lights came down onto the road surface to reveal Zeke spread out as if on a drying rack, but in the middle of the road.

"Holy fuck!" said Clewesy as he swung hard toward the edge of the road. We hit the bushes, and the car stalled. But we had both heard the double thump as the car had passed over Zeke. I looked over and Clewesy had collapsed on the steering wheel, weeping, "I've killed me mate! I killed me fucking mate."

I was quite sober at this point but couldn't open my door as the car was jammed against bushes. So I crawled through into the back and left through the driver's side rear. On the road I couldn't see and yelled at Clewesy to bring the car around and shine the lights up the road. He did.

Zeke was there in exactly the same position as he had been before we hit him, except his left arm was across his chest instead of straight out. I could see rocks and gravel embedded into his skin so I picked some off and noticed that his arm was badly swollen. We decided to take him to the hospital, as we had surely broken his arm.

Now he had to be lifted into the car into the back seat. Too heavy and big to get in properly, we put him part way in and pushed the rest in as we closed the door. Aimlessly driving for some time and punctuated occasionally by Zeke yelling, "Where's me fucking rifle?", we were guided by providence to a hospital sign.

After parking, Clewesy went to the door and announced that he had run over his mate and surely broken his arm. People came wheeling a bed, I opened the door of the car and Zeke shot out like he was spring-loaded. He landed head first on the gravel with his legs still on the back seat. Oh, fuck it, I thought; let the professionals deal with it. I stepped back. They lowered the bed, loaded Zeke and went in.

After closing the car door I followed, gave details at the desk to a sleepy-looking young man and sat down. I dozed off, waking as the doctor arrived.

"Oh, shit, this could go wrong," I thought. "He's Chinese." No trouble; he took the swollen arm and gently removed gravel, cleaned and dressed it.

As the doctor stood up, Zeke's eyes opened. He screamed as he swung a wild fist, "You fucking slope, I'll fucking kill you!"

The doctor stepped back and allowed Zeke's momentum to carry him to the floor, where he lay without moving further. The doctor said to someone, "Help me straighten him up and we will leave him here where he won't fall any further." Fairly cool, I thought.

I started to get up to help, and to apologise to the doctor, when Clewesy woke with a snort, saw Zeke on the floor with the little doctor pushing him, and ran across the room screaming, "Don't you fucking hit my mate, you prick!" He leapt onto the doctor's back and bit his head. I pulled him off before any damage was done and explained what had happened.

Clewesy sat down, crying and saying "sorry" over and over again to the doctor, who, very decently I felt, thought we might like to leave soon as Zeke's arm was too swollen to be X-rayed; and that maybe we could go for an X-ray somewhere more local to us, in a few days' time. We drove to the base and took Zeke to his room. Not noticing his stuff was gone, we put him on his bed and left.

Clewesy and I made the 6:00am parade and lined up according to height, so he was too distant to talk to, just wave. After a bit of drill, roll call happened; alphabetical, so I was late in the order. Administration knew that Zeke had missed the truck to the funny country so had put his name back on the platoon list. He was last. As names were called we answered with a crisp "Sir!" to indicate presence.

"Wight."

"Sir!"

"Younger."

"Sir!"

"Zaffino."

Nothing.

Again. Still nothing.

The Sergeant yelled, "Anyone who knows the whereabouts of Private Zaffino, prove!" To prove meant to bend your right arm at right angles with the hand pointing stiffly forward. I did so. Clewes too.

I was closer, so the Sergeant came to stand in front of me. He was a proper soldier; Vietnam more than once, lean, brown, and his uniform fitted beautifully.

He leaned forward, and in my ear, with a quiet voice of purest gravel, he said, "Private Wight. You look particularly disgusting this morning, more like a bag of shit tied in the middle every time I see you. Now speak to me of Private Zaffino."

As softly as possible I said, "Private Clewes and I ran over Private Zaffino early this morning."

The Sergeant leaned back again and gazed directly at me. Many seconds passed and I swear he began to smile.

"Thank you, Private Wight, I don't expect to hear better news than that all day."

He sharply turned, crisply marched, and stamped to a stop in front of Lieutenant Filewood, a National Service officer – a species held in the highest disdain by proper soldiers.

I realised why the Sergeant had smiled. He gave a sharp salute and, at the top of his voice, reported, "Private Wight and Private Clewes have run over Private Zaffino, sir."

A laugh spread across the parade ground. The Lieutenant was going to be hard put to bring good order back. Then, as if on cue, the door to the barracks opened up behind him and, in full view of all but the officer no longer in charge, stood Zeke, naked and squinting out into the sunlight.

He had been ill since I had seen him. Barely vertical, he put his bandaged arm up to his eyes and said loud enough for all to hear, "Piss off, you pack of bastards." And closed the door.

The remaining coherence of that piece of Australia's military machine collapsed. Several men were on their knees and one pissed himself.

It was minutes before we were soldiers again, but the damage was done. We all knew we were pretending.

# MAX'S CD PLAYER

*D*riving. On the road to Max's place and excited today, as I bear a gift.

I have discovered that The Grateful Dead are available on CD. I am sure that if I lived in the world properly I would have found them long ago. Maybe not. If I lived in the world properly I would not have looked in their direction. Still, Kombi in full song and me too, and Jerry playing; it's all feeling good.

Closer to the lake I turn inland a little and arrive, to see Max sitting. I have turned the music off, and will speak of it after the cup of tea. Max is well he says, and admires the van, as the windows are recently tinted and you can't see in the back from outside anymore. "Not that there is anything to steal, just bedding and a change of clothes."

Max nods. "Mate, if you can't stop in the city, get in the back, make tea and have a nap without anyone knowing, then your van isn't finished."

Unable to wait, I say I have some Dead to play, reach in and extract the CD from the player, realising as I do so that there is something to steal after all. I wave it at Max.

"I don't have a player for that, mate. I don't like them much."

I am astonished. I like the module. It is more robust and seems, in every way that I can think of, vastly superior to vinyl. Still there must be a reason, so I ask.

"Long story, mate. Cup of tea first, and then I will tell all."

Sitting a little while later, drinking it, I remind him of the story waiting. Max takes a breath and begins.

"You know Ravi Shankar?"

I nod. He goes on, "Yehudi Menuhin?"

More nodding.

"Well, they heard about it too and thought it sounded like a real good idea, so they arranged a digital recording session together so they could check it out properly."

I like the story so far and wonder aloud what they would have recorded.

"I don't know, mate, but they hated it. Yehudi said it was like a musical corpse. Seemed right, no life. Clear and crisp, but dead. Ravi had the same reaction."

I wonder. I don't hear that in it, it sounds fine to me; but those two are among the finest musicians in the world. One assumes they have some idea.

Max goes on. "They decided that it was because the waveform had been removed and that it had taken the sound integrity away. If you listen to vinyl or tapes, the noise you hear has always been in a waveform, never in numbers. Analogue, not digital."

"Well, they might know. I don't feel bad with it, though."

Max sips tea and says, "I don't hear it either, but I can't see electricity and that can affect me."

"Mate, Christians say that about Satan. It doesn't have legs."

"Maybe, but the whole digital business is a bother to me and I'll hold off as long as I can, or at least until I can get it clear in my mind."

I don't understand what he is finding hard here. Music? Well, that could be decided on current thinking, but I can make little sense of 'the whole digital business' he is talking about. Neil comes up the driveway and is made a cup of tea. We sit to drink.

I can't let it go, so I ask Max about his problem with it all. Neil answers instead.

"Mate, your VW, what is wrong with it?"

"Not much," I say. "The brakes need adjusting, and I might put an electric fuel pump in. The old one is a bit dodgy. I'm carrying the new one in the car in case it gives up completely."

"So, how do you know that?"

"The pedal is closer to the floor, mate, all adjustable by pulling on the handbrake."

"All the stuff in it is sequential and dependent in a linear way on other bits, right?"

I nod.

"So when something goes wrong it shows up in nearby systems, it is all leaning on the next bits; and, if you know, failures cast a shadow before them, fault deductible by form."

"Okay, I get it. What is the point here?"

"Well, digital stuff is the opposite. It just goes or stops. All or nothing. One thing goes wrong in a mobile phone, it is all over. In the bin and get another one. At best you need to replace some whole module because one tiny bit went wrong."

We have travelled a fair distance from the music problem; I figure the two of them were being Luddites, so I say so.

"Not so, mate. We've both got good high-end computing, and use it; it just goes where it doesn't belong. It is a completely different way of thinking."

"Silicon," says Max.

"That's it. We produce devices all ordered and able to be interfaced at any point by people; the computing is the opposite. Your car is an analogue, carbon-based, thinker's device. The computer is silicon thinking, different and unapproachable in the normal manner. Modules that you can't interface decently with."

"I get it, guys; I just don't see why it's important, except that you like carbon-based music better."

Max suggests that we go to the pub at this point and get a beer to hold onto, and we can bang the table with our free hands as we speak. Also buy a meal, as it will be time to eat soon. We walk; it is nice, late afternoon in spring, cool and clear. At the pub, we nod to people and move to a table near the windows overlooking the lake. Max is at the bar buying us a drink.

"Have you two talked at length about this?" I ask Neil.

"Yes, mate. The damn stuff is like a virus and is moving into societal systems where I reckon it's totally destructive."

"How's that? I mean, it is just a tool, and a damn good one."

"I use it all the time. I generate documents, keep track of dollars, send email and use the Net to look up all kinds of useful stuff. It's brilliant and it's the way to use a modular system, so efficient and so clear. Digital and silicone. What's a bugger about it is that that very efficiency is now seen as the final and only proper way to behave in almost every business and Government agency I have seen in ages."

I get a glimpse of this; I drink beer and thank Max, who seems content to let Neil go on.

"Tell me more, mate."

"Look. Remember where we worked?"

I do. We were both clerically occupied at a rehabilitation place run by the Government that assisted the damaged to come back into the world. A nice thing to do, I say.

"It was good, we were able to help lots of people, all the departments worked together and people were the centre of it all. We used to make special efforts here and there to make it work for them."

I buy beer and sit again.

Neil continues. "The point is, that is not possible now. In the name of the modular, silicone-style efficiency it is all in its little sections, minimally staffed and very specifically task-driven. Defined activities only and pity the poor bugger who comes in the door with a problem that doesn't fit exactly into the descriptor. They will die in the ditch. People are not the centre of it now, the efficiency of the system is."

He drinks. Good thing too, I think. I need a moment. That is all I get as he puts his beer down. "Even if the staff *wants* to assist, they can't. There aren't enough of them now to be flexible, and they are forced into modular behaviour as a person and section."

"Were you guys off your face when you worked this out?"

I see the efficient face of economic rationalism, and the modular tidiness of it all. The inhumanity of it is real, but I can't lay it all at the feet of computing.

Max agrees, but goes on to say that it doesn't matter who or what is to blame, the evolution of form in society into efficient modules, fit in or perish, has happened, and computers mirror it. We have to function inside the digitized form or we are outside the system and its benefits. The cost, he thinks, is humanity in pretty well any interaction. He concludes by saying that the first time he had talked about this, yes, he was well off his face.

I thought so. There is a flavour about stoned-think, but that doesn't make it all false.

"We are pretty well fucked really," I say. "We can't confront it as the efficiencies of system defence are very high, and you would be arrested or put in a home for the bewildered. What do you do other than limiting your computer use to human functions, not buying CD players and grumping in the pub?"

Silence. Neil goes off to buy the next beers. He comes back grinning.

"I just did it."

"What?" I ask.

"I asked the bartender module how he was, did he live local. He does, and is studying. What? I said. Engineering, he said. I spoke of mathematics, mentioned slide rules and the log book. He has never seen either one. I am going to bring them in and show him."

"Did what?" I ask again.

"Look at him," says Neil.

I turn toward the barman; he waves to us and smiles.

Neil says, "See? I was human. Nobody does it anymore, but he liked it. So what we can do is spike the system at the interface points. Remind people of what was; some don't even remember nice strangers. To the battle, be nice to every bored checkout person and every single poor sod in a deathly boring job. It won't work of course, but I will feel better if I behave like carbon and not silicone."

I look at Max. He looks back, and says, "If not us mate, then who?"

# THE WORLD DOESN'T WORK

*Did you need proof, really?*

*U*ntil recently, every time that someone in the world played Rachmaninov publicly, his granddaughter got free money. She has an island of her own.

Driving in America along a sort of linear highway city, cruising really, almost daydreaming, but not quite. Suddenly the boxy 4wd in front of me stopped. Just screamed to a halt, right there.

Instantly. No chance for me to stop at all.

In the USA there is a brilliant thing that isn't for this type of moment at all, but it helped. It is a centre lane. For turning from only, so you can't travel in it, but as you turn, not clog up the highway. I swung the car hard into it and missed the stopped box by a miracle of the first water. Lots of adrenalin, all fired up, I managed to stop right next to the car that had skidded to a halt so precipitously. I glared at the tinted passenger window. Jesus suffering fuck. Bastard, I thought, what did you do that for? As the window came electrically down, I was ready. A grandma rancher woman with a grey hair bun appeared and said: "Well done, young man. Fine driving there. I had to stop; I couldn't believe you missed me." I didn't see that coming.

It happened to a mate in some South American country, as he rode a rented motorbike down a mountain dirt track. He was pretending to be a young Che Guevara in his own youth-recapturing mode, I am sure. As he saw a little restaurant, he belatedly noticed the log on the road and lost the bike side-ways in avoidance.

Now Phil has had a bike forever and so, at about fifty miles an hour, he dropped it on its side and sat on it as it slid to a halt. He got up, stood the bike up, twisted things back some and walked toward the restaurant. There was a Rasta-style bloke sitting outside, a massive dreaded hairpile under a knitted coloured thing and a fat joint in hand. He already had a second beer on the table, pushed it to Phil and said, "Very aware riding, mahn."

In India at an ashram that had safety deposit box facilities,I needed a small photograph to identify myself. A trip into town and there was a 'Two-Hour Photographs' studio near the main street for my convenience. A great deal of sitting and curtain arrangement followed, peppered with glasses of chai and fine conversation until finally a photo-graph was taken. I paid. I then thanked the operator as he gave me a receipt and told me to come back on Thursday, four days hence. I was amazed. I directed his attention to his large sign offering me two-hour service, and he smiled politely and said: "Oh no, sir, you are mistaken. There are several photographs yet to be used on my film. However, when I place it with my friend the processor on Thursday morning, it will return in only two hours!"

I taught design for years to high school students. As an introduction at around 12 years old in Year 8, they were grouped and given a box with a specific selection of straws, chopsticks, glue and tape, a knife, things like that. Also a large glass marble. The task was simple: to use the material in the box to support the marble as close to the ceiling as possible. I had been warned that in this class a behaviour problem of the first order was to be present and to be aware that he could go wrong. He did look surly. As I was intro-ducing the task, he suddenly became aware of what was required, reached into the box and took the marble, stood on the bench and taped it to the ceiling. I loved it and got everybody to stand and clap.

I went to Ground Zero. It was Saturday afternoon and lots of people were there. Some places carry the knowing of themselves totally, The Chapel of the Holy Cross in Sedona is one, this was another. It was brownie-thick with grief and shocked anguish. Tears just came for every gaspingly horrible loss anyone has ever had.

I walked down a side street after awhile and figured out why the firemen were on the ball that day. They are the neighbours. A fireman with a thick Irish accent was there guiding a truck backwards out through people, I felt at home with him as Australia is a bit Irish, "Gedday, Paddy howsit goin'?" He looked at me. After a while he said, "You're Australian aren't ye?" "Yes, mate." No denying it really. Another pause. "Well then, boyo, you can stay. The rest of these people, tell them to feck off."

I saw Osho a number of times, lots really. He saw me twice that I know of. First time after a journey of years of not making it and disappointment I did it in America by the skin of my wallet. There was a drive-by to happen in the afternoon and I couldn't wait. I was early on the road all alone and shocked as the crowd thickened and shoved me round jockeying for position. I held my place, and finally saw the Rolls coming. As I looked at him closing, he suddenly turned and looked me right in the eyes, I saw him smile and nod for a thousand years, the world simply collapsed, then he was past. I couldn't move, breathe or stop weeping. My friends held me up all the way back to the rooms. I may never have recovered.

Sixteen sessions of physical therapy with a mad big Italian called Ananto. A sort of rebalancing. Massively effective for the body over the weeks. We were friends through my girlfriend and got on fine. He would walk up to me often

– we were living in an ashram – and pull my moustache or beard. Hard! It was excruciatingly painful. Weeks it went on for, I spoke to him and avoided him but daily there he was. I was standing outside before lunch after weeks of this, I had had a session with him that morning, a fine one too. He stood and pulled my moustache, I squared and powered a punch into his body. I felt it sink in deep. As he sank down he had tears from pain I was sure. I helped him up, he looked at me and said, "And about time too."

Ross bought a house. He had to because his girlfriend had taken the last one away. The new back yard was filled with opium poppies, so I harvested them rightly and decided to take them to Peter's for tea making. On a bus. A big plastic bag full, as we were two weeks on holiday.

All was well until about a hundred miles from where I was to get off. Someone left their wallet in the toilet and returned to get it an hour later to find it missing. The bus driver sensibly locked down the bus and searched the flushings of the toilet, found the wallet, but without money or cards in. He then rang the police to meet us where I was to disembark. My contraband was in the hold so I felt fine.

The police of course were late. I asked to be searched so I could go to my ride, they did, but poorly. I helped by taking my shoes off and turning my pockets inside out. "You know about this, mate?" I told them I used to do security for the Dalai Lama. That was helpful I am sure. Still no police and I was given my opiate bag from within and sent on my way.

Peter was nowhere to be seen. The police arrived and I panicked. I rang him and said to get here fast and get me out of the place as there was serious trouble. "Two minutes, mate, on way." Nice. He didn't even ask. As the bus driver pointed me out to the police it was clear that they were interested in searching me properly, and now I had a bag from inside that will get looked in too. Ah, bugger, he's coming.

Right then the big and suitably impressive company car turned in and pulled up next to me hard, screeching tyres and digging in at the front. Peter got out, slamming. He had gone to the trouble of putting on a sleeveless tee shirt and looked very surly indeed. Doom was abundant. He saw the policeman coming and faced him directly smiling. "Hi Geoff, what's happening?" My mate the Managing Director. All about us relaxed, and after a short conversation in which I was confirmed as an old hippie mate and definitely not a thief, we left. Peter wanted details. I promised to tell him everything over a nice cup of tea.

I had returned from India with Ross to an airport near Peter's, and we were to be there for his 40th birthday. I had bought two absurdly ballistic skyrocket fireworks for the occasion in India and would set them off as the night began to peak. In customs a very young man approached us and asked how we had paid for our tickets. He had a customs tag on his neck so I told him a tale of American Express. He didn't care for it and invited us to "Follow the red line, please." When my bag was opened I was further invited regarding my 'explosives' to wait in a small room. Grilled for two hours and threatened with fines and prison by one Constable Creek, I had my fireworks confiscated and was told to go. Peter and Ross were waiting in the empty airport. It turned out that, even though they hadn't met, they were both from the same part of the Port and had ridden in seriously opposing biker clubs. Ross didn't remember Peter; he remembered his bike, and gave me a seriously hard time for smashing it thirty years before.

A Richie Havens concert. Why not. And a front row seat too. He is something else it turned out, I remember him from the Woodstock movie. The concert was different, so mellow and filled with joy. His clothes were plain and Nehru style, and he was quieter than I had imagined.

There was someone crazy interrupting all through, sudden references to Jesus and God, loud and freaky. She was out of it, some distance from what was going on. All around me people were getting real pissed off. After the closing number she stood and walked forward to the stage and let a tirade of earnest sinful accusation fly at him. He stopped, put his guitar back on, stood as close as he could and sang the most beautiful love song to her right there. After, he leaned forward and put his guitar pick into her hand and squeezed it gently closed, smiled long to her and left. Nice man; nicer than me that day.

# GET A JOB

*"It is when the Gods hate a man with particular abomination,*
*that they thrust upon him the profession of schoolmaster."*

(Nero's tutor)

This morning, because I was late, entirely to do with my proper and full-blown addiction to good coffee, I fucked up big time. No real harm done, but I have gone from total credibility to damage control.

I hate it.

At school in time to drink coffee and check the temporary teacher paperwork thoroughly, instead I drank coffee, quickly arranged the papers in order and spent the time gained looking at a mate's new computer. Hardly worth the trouble really, a tiny Macintosh notebook. A PowerBook 100 with fuck-all of anything, attractive only because Mac software is tiny and elegant enough to run decently on a system with 4 meg of ram and a 70 Meg hard disk.

So it has come to pass that in first lesson I am in a bus with two classes of kids on the way to the local swimming pool so they can learn to swim. A dream start. I will catch up the paperwork properly and sit under a tree for an hour. Easy.

We arrive, they change into swimming gear, and I begin the courteous changeover of responsibility to the swimming pool staff, one of who asks me for the medical declarations. I have never heard of these. I will seek advice. The pool staff wait in silence.

110

My mobile phone is in a no-signal area, so I ring the school on someone's portable. This brings me to the reception desk of the school; proper, nice people. I ask for the guy whose lesson I am taking. "Sorry, he has just left." Of course he has, that's why I am replacing him. I ask for the Deputy Principal.

These papers I need are a legal requirement. A little arse-cover in case of medical emergency. "I have a certificate signed by his parent saying that he needs no medication, thus I cannot be held responsible for his insulin-deprivation coma."

Total crap of course. No such thing has ever happened and doubtless never will – unless this particular lesson goes ahead without this particular paperwork; and then of course, every student will be comatose in moments.

Back on the phone, I look guiltily at the students whose swimming break is disappearing and the looming pool staff immovables that dare me to not locate the paperwork, and are threatening to enter "teachers are fuckwits" mode.

Everybody in the western world has opinions about teachers. They all went to school for years and many are filled with tales of horror and personal torture. Some rejoice in the telling of a sweetly vengeful moment tormenting and humiliating some teacher – a fuckwit, of course.

I want only to see them in front of a class of students who want to learn something and laughingly watch them collapse as the pressure for clarity from young, fast minds crushes them.

Now the Deputy Principal is on the phone. No I don't have them, I assume that George has them. No they won't go ahead without. Yes, go and look in his office.

I wait. I look organised; all the paperwork for the day lined up like cascading windows on a PC on the poolside table, bag, phone, pen and notebook computer. All meaningless without the medical declarations. No, not meaningless; they prove to the assembled bronzed Gods and Goddesses currently pretending to be swimming instructors that the condiments of teacher wankerdom, as suspected, are nothing more than a veneer to hide total incompetence.

I could have done some work. Now it will be storyteller to these students until the bus arrives. Ah, well I won't mind that and they won't either. Still, it's not a swimming lesson.

The papers are not in George's office. No, don't send the bus early; I will take care of it. I don't want to piss the bus driver off as well. I hang up. Ten minutes of waiting; it's enough – crowd control time.

I reach for the folder with the student roll in it and it spills everywhere. Fuck! Can it get worse? Of course it can. The folder has opened and spewed papers all over. The pool staff recognise them immediately.

"There they are!" I hand twenty medical declarations over to the blonde flagpole and notice that all her junior staff are looking up to heaven. I apologise to the kids for the delay. They don't seem to mind.

Everybody else will.

# ATHENA AND CARMEL

*You realize that time is seriously passing when you*
*have dead ex-lovers.*

*D*riving on an early Saturday morning to a Greek Ortho-
dox Church. An old friend is dead.

I don't go to funerals much. More now that I am older,
but still not much. The first problem is what to wear – special
occasion clothes are a thing of my childhood. But this one is
different, so I bought something. I really loved Athena and
she liked things right, so I went and bought a sort of loose
trouser and blousy shirt. All white, for some reason. I hate
shopping for clothes now. Shop assistants are all children
who lie about what you look like and think you are a bit odd.

Athena was a Transcendental Meditation teacher, one of
those in the first group ever taught in India by Maharishi
Mahesh Yogi. I learned it from her in the late Sixties sometime. Unlike the TM movement now, then you got quite
amazing after-sales service when you took your fruit, handkerchief and comparatively few dollars to swap for a mantra.

We were a dramatic lot, prone to freaking out, paranoia
and the fruits of narcissism – or just being fucked up on bad
drugs. The time of day or night irrelevant, I and many others
just fronted up to her door more than once in some state of
mental disarray, to be made welcome with Greek sweets,
short, strong coffee, and a listener without equal. After that,
a bed made; then in the morning, breakfast. You can't respect
that enough. So, I suffered the clothes purchasing.

I had known she was dying for some time and decided not to visit. Every time I thought about it I could hear her saying, "So twenty-five years – we never see you. Now I am dying, you come." I knew there was no proper answer to that, so I stayed away.

So, here I am. At five minutes before the 10am start, I arrive at the church and park my old Ford in some small underground car park at the back. Around the front and at the door is an array of old TM practitioners all in white blousy clothes, and TM teachers in suits. I am made welcome by everyone. We are older, but that's all. Nothing else seems different. I feel pleased to be recognised and sort of belonging to a group again.

Inside the church the walls are all painted with saints and halos in bright colours. I am enjoying this very much when Al comes to sit next to me. I want to jump up and hug him, but am being funereal.

Al is one of the nicest people in the world. His little beard is gone, but his eyes are still alight. He seems, as always, to be an active member of some church that joyously looks upon everything as if God is about to jump out from behind it and surprise us all. Peter describes him as 'the only person I know who seems to be just naturally wise.' Al is a joy. I speak, he answers; and I hear from his voice that he is tremendously shaken. Lots of people love Athena.

I look up as someone goes to the pulpit and looks ready to speak. He starts after realising nobody was going to stop talking until he did. He talks about Athena being born in Egypt and migrating here, about five languages and translating for people in trouble, about social work, much loved by all, and general 'she sounds nice but I didn't know her' funeral priest talk.

At the end he gives the floor to Jeff, an ancient meditator, who gently describes her from the soul outward. We all love it. Then there is a sort of walk past the coffin, nice photo on top, taken about the time I knew her best, and deep silence in the place as we move slowly along. Al is in front of me in the line, very quiet, a namaste palms together salute – and then out the side door. I do the same, speak my thanks to Athena in Hindi, and with rolling tears, follow Al's exit. He makes his apologies, invites me to go visit him and leaves. I will, too; I haven't seen him for ages.

The rest of us move into a nearby outbuilding, where there is a beautiful European feast set out on long tables. So we eat. All sublime as expected. I have a little trouble at funerals changing gear into social mode straight after, and so am awkward for a while with everybody. Maybe I should do what Al did; just go.

Barbara is there, an old lover, talking loudly and with confidence, seeming successful in the 90's way. Somehow I don't believe it, God knows why. I don't trust her. Everybody is old friend-ish and I am feeling a bit 'moment before an accident', all separate and distant.

Then I am stunned with the joy of hearing Carmel laugh in the back of the room. All rich and full; a lovely earthy woman, properly pagan. I stand up to look. Then I remember that she is dead too. Ah, fuckitall.

Looking anyway, I see Kate, Carmel's twin sister. Looks nothing like her, but laughs exactly the same. Already shaken, now I am thrown completely. I go to see Kate and get a giant 'pleased to see you hug' and am asked if I am okay. "Well, I was just doing alright until I heard you laugh."

She interrupts me, sounding a bit hurt; "I don't think Athena would have minded a bit."

"No, no, I'm sure of that. It's because you sound like Carmel." I can feel tears moving down my cheeks again. Kate wipes one and says, "She loved you a lot, man."

"I know, she told me. I miss her today, you know. Now."

I knew Carmel loved me. I loved her, too. Petite, and alcoholic, and with little confidence in herself, still she was one of the brave people who always looked me in the eyes and told the truth.

Years ago, not long after I had first met her, she rang me and said to come visit. When I arrived she asked if I would be her lover. Shit, I didn't know what to say. She went on to explain that, after a while without one, she always got drunk and grabbed the first man who would come home with her. A few very bad mornings and a bit of a stalking later, she thought she needed a regular lover, a friend whom she could ring up to go places and sleep with when she felt like it. I said yes, that would be nice, and we went to bed just for fun. For years, according to circumstance, we were friends, companions and lovers.

Somehow we lost touch. Carmel drank. I went to India. When I came back she had moved. Gone. Not in the phone book, her mother not sure, Kate interstate and unfindable. Too hard.

Some years later I was being a social isolate. It was the 31st of December and all around me people were merry-making for New Year's Eve. I ran into Kate at the city market, we chatted, and she directed me to Carmel hiding in a cottage in the hills.

That afternoon I drove along ever-narrowing roads and tracks, to finally arrive at a fence covered in blackberries and a gap just big enough to squeeze through. Old fruit trees. A tiny white cottage with vines and a little verandah. All a bit run down. I knocked and heard movement behind the door.

Carmel opened it. She had lost weight, thin with jeans and T-shirt. Still nice-looking, but a bit haunted. She was glad to see me, and we had tea, no milk. No fridge, you see, and not liking to see people much she didn't use the supermarket unless she had to.

There wasn't much food. I invited myself to eat and went to the shop for stuff. Carmel hadn't planned anything for New Year, so this was okay with her. I asked if wine was okay, too. "Why not?" she thought out loud, grinning; "it's New Year's Eve."

I spent extra for a bottle of nice Shiraz, cigarettes too; then I cooked. We drank and laughed a lot, filled in the gaps, and then went to bed. It was all lovely. Next morning, after we ate toast and drank coffee, I left. When I went back a few weeks later she wasn't there. That was the last time I saw her.

I say to Kate, "I was in Tasmania teaching when she died. I didn't know until I got back months later. I went to the cemetery, just a little brass plate in the ground in among dozens of others. I stood on top of it, trying to get close. Not warm. Nothing growing."

I am crying again.

Kate was there when Carmel died of pneumonia on the floor of their shared flat. She said not to bring the ambulance; she just wanted to go home. So Kate didn't and Carmel went.

Twins. I reckon they have rights with each other.

Kate is looking at me cry, comes close for a big hug, then we cry together a little.

She says, "Hey man, we are getting old. People we love are dying."

# WHY BOTHER (2)

*"I don't want your wings,*
*I don't want your freedom in a lie"*
Donovan – Turquoise

*P*eter sent me a copy of one of Richard Neville's books, the ones that recall and comment on the Sixties as he saw them from London.

The book came with a note that simply said, "Read this." I felt a bit like *Alice in Wonderland*. I trust his judgment, so I began with interest.

Shit, I hated it. It's like finding yourself on a Macintosh computer when you're a PC user. Enough things are in place so it seems familiar, but there is some deep and abiding foreignness about it that gets further and further up your nose. Of course, when you're asked, all you can say is "Well... it's just... wrong."

This perception seemed a little simplistic, so I let it sit a few days, then read some more. The same. I rang Peter.

"I am the same. That's why I sent it to you, bro, with this conversation in mind."

We talked a while, got nowhere. I let it sit another day and went to the city and bought more Richard Neville books.

I read them. The same feeling. Looks like food but it's not. Some literary hamburger franchise has begun to homogenise published writings. This theory was clearly wrong as I noticed that all his books, even the early ones, affected me thus. In fact, they pissed me off the most. Is this just a jealous

118

guarding of territory or a refusal to accept another's use of the same symbolism in a different way? I was glad the early ones annoyed me more; this gave me something to reason with.

As usual in these matters of intuition, the thinking was of little use. My past experience told me that an understanding always follows the intuitive leap if you pay attention and wait awhile. I read more and waited.

This whole situation puzzled me deeply. On the surface I was sure that I would be overjoyed in these non-hippie times to find coherent reference to ways of the Sixties. How come the opposite was happening?

Lying in bed, drifting, it fell on me from a great height. I grabbed the nearest book and just the cover was enough. The book was called *Out of my mind* and the cover featured Richard sitting on some kind of Nepalese golden throne. He was a publisher in the Sixties, a master of publicity, a businessman, then and now exploiting his presence in those times. He probably can't believe his luck.

No real risk even then for Richard – with business and parental safety-net always beneath, inheritance of consequence, friends of influence on side, all waiting. He was learning the language of the day, gathering concepts, following fashionable trends, all to turn the times into dollars and slake the ego as though a Rosetta stone between the Sixties and now. He is now, as always, a straight man in business with a cultivated product to sell.

No wonder it tastes like cardboard and offends me so. It looks like a place where you can get a good down-home meal and a dose of the contentment that follows. Instead, you are treated to the egoistic ramblings of a man who takes the jewellery of the time and decorates his bank account with it.

I rang Peter.

He said, "Why don't *you* write one? You're a born raver."

Fuck it. I will, I thought.

# FOUL PAL AL GETS HIT BY THE PSYCHIC BUS

*I said I would visit, now I have...*

*I*t's a fine spring mid-morning, early coffee has been quietly consumed and a trip to the Botanic Gardens is in order. I will sit there and read for a while and look at the passing parade.

As I get in the van I think of Al. It is months since I saw him at Athena's funeral and I did promise to go see him. We could both go to the gardens and sit and talk under a tree. I like the picture in my mind and turn the van around.

I wonder why I imagine anyone will be home, as realisation comes that it is a weekday. Oh well, I will leave a note. In a nearby green, tree-lined suburb, I turn down the street and look for the distinctive fence with the big vines draping. The roses are starting in the front of the garden, other plants look good with rocks; no front lawn, I see.

At the door now, and it seems someone is home as the main door is open and the security door is ajar slightly. I knock. Al answers. He looks terrible. I mean, really terrible. He is haggard, his face is scratched and bruised, he is round shouldered – and his eyes dart about. None of this is like him.

"Ah, thank God it's *you*, mate. I nearly didn't answer."

"What's happening, Al? Are you going to be okay?"

"I dunno, mate. Come in."

Inside I hug him and he starts to cry. I am shipwrecked by sudden change but somehow centred in the face of all this.

He says he will make tea and I go with him to help. When we sit, he tells me what happened. He doesn't remember the main part, but is sure he went to a party the night before, drank quite a bit, and then lost consciousness. Some memory of a taxicab and yelling at people who were yelling at him. Not much to work with other than he has clearly taken a beating.

"How did you get home, mate?" It seems a good question, as we are playing detective.

"I woke up by the river this morning early and rang Jane from a phone box. She came and got me."

Al and Jane have been married forever and carry it better than any couple I know. She must be worried, I think to myself.

"She was all over the place, mate," he says, as though I had asked out loud. "Really glad to see me. None of the questions she had every right to ask. God I was grateful."

"Where is she, mate?"

"I told her I was all right, so she went to get the car from the party site. I'm glad you came. I am probably not all right."

I agree. He is close to tears again. Whatever has happened here is so out of context with the kindly life Al seems to lead that I am sure he can't be easy with it. The house is light and delicate with post-hippie stuff here and there. Wedding photos. Al and Jane alight with love in some trees – he with beard and round glasses, and she with long hair and cheese-cloth in the sunlight. Nothing here to put today in context.

We talk some more, and it comes to light that the night before Al had more to drink than usual. "Work stress," he says.

I believe it too. He has been school counsellor at an inner city high school for ten years at least. A job like that is burn-out material in a couple of years. When I say so he agrees and thinks that it might have something to do with it all.

"The real problem here, mate, is that I don't remember anything. I can't get a context to handle it with. That is what is freaking me out! I have bruises and marks, I remember running and hiding near the river, and people were after me – and that's all."

"And the taxi."

"Yeah, and the taxi."

We have more tea and are quiet a long time.

"Work has been real bad in the last couple of weeks too." Al leans back in his recently occupied chair. Until a minute ago we were sitting on the front step.

"I've got two kids going right off. One is the son of the people who own the coffee shop you hang out in. He is stealing money in quantity from the business and using it at school in all kinds of bent ways. His parents are not pleased, but we are getting there.

"As well as him, there is this proper little thug who thumps younger kids and will only stop for money. His parents are rough buggers and they definitely do not like schoolteachers or the middle class and in particular *me*, who is both. I want this kid out of the school. They are resisting in every way possible."

I wonder how it is possible to resist under the circumstances but don't ask, as a car comes in the driveway. It is Jane. We speak of Al, the kids, make fresh tea and sit again. Jane has an appointment to keep and is clearly very pleased I am here to keep Al company.

We find ourselves outside, at the back of the house, left alone with a light lunch and white wine, all made manifest by Jane in the moment before she left. Not bad, I think. We eat quietly and then lean back with the wine and feel good.

Smiling, Al says, "I was thinking of taking up the vacancy in outdoor education. A bit of quiet abseiling and mountain climbing; you know, with death right at your shoulder where you can see the bugger."

Al has always bushwalked and has a nice old four-wheel drive for desert and mountain holidays. We spent a very fine few days in the late Sixties among the ranges, north, driving through impossible terrain in a pair of old, split-window VW vans, to a gorge walk of great beauty.

I remind him of these things and suggest that he is more than properly qualified for the job. He thinks so too. "I can get it if I want, or be computing senior."

"Now *there* is a job to have, Al. All air-conditioned and kids wanting to know what you have to teach. A very good choice indeed. Use your holidays to go bush and balance it all up."

"I might! No belligerent and threatening parents in that part of the curriculum."

"Do you get nasty ones much, mate?"

Al looks at me directly. "Mate, the father of the standover thug, a huge bastard and built like a brick shithouse, had his face next to mine across the desk telling me that he was going to take the trouble to find me and beat the life out of me in no uncertain terms. That was only a few days ago. I have been terrified. I can't sleep; can't deal with it at all."

"Quite the opposite of death at your shoulder, some sneaky bastard coming up to king-hit you when you are not paying attention."

"You know what I thought this morning, mate?" I don't, and say so.

"I thought that the aggravation of all this might be too much. So rather than stay with it, I got lost inside where the fear of beatings lives; dissociated and went away to be beaten because that was easier than waiting."

It sounds coherent to me, but what a mess. Even in the knowing, Al still seems shaken and lost, hurting from top to bottom.

"That's a good place to start, mate. Get out of it. Take another job."

"I'll take a few weeks off first, and then we will see. But whatever, I won't do that again. I'll take a break before it comes unstuck."

We finish the wine, and doze off under the tree.

And then Al decides to take a break.

# LETTER FROM MY FATHER

*I had a mate who lost it before he died, knew nobody,*
*remembered nothing. I felt he was in a nice place*
*so I imagined this.*

on,

This is my last letter. I know you well enough to be sure
that you will understand why, not because I don't love you
deeply, but that I won't be here to write.

This letter is to reassure you in moments of doubt as to
my sanity.

I have been fighting the final let-go for months now, but
the tastes that I have had of rich, free wanderings is too much;
and soon I will go and may never find myself here again.

Being old is quite an experience, but let me assure you,
you will lose nothing, and I mean *nothing* inside, as the years
are softly lost to your work and family.

The shock of finding your hair thinner and your beard
grey is nothing. As I sit here I am the same man who went
to war as an old soldier forty years ago; not one thing has
changed. My mind is still in the same places and moves the
same paths, has wonderful lustful thoughts when appreciat-
ing the beautiful women here.

Only one thing is changed and I realise that with shock
when I look in a mirror – my body has gone! There is in
my place an ancient man, shaking and weak, but I still live
inside, as I always have.

With the movement of the body to this state, the link

to the world becomes slowly less. There is no need for it, of course; I have nothing to do. Not even feed myself if I don't want to! The world fades, the immediate has depth unimaginable. The pleasure of the simple, the folds in my bedspread fill my mind totally, so rich with light fondling and caverns within.

You, too, will remember later that this is the same as your childhood.

I seem to be unwinding.

What comes next I feel beautifully safe with, as though I am going home. Immense relief is there and tears of joy come as I feel the thought bring the reality close, as though a taste in my mouth.

How, my love, can I tell you, the children and your beautiful friend Joanne that I am perfectly okay, when your every fibre will scream no!

I found myself yesterday walking in Budapest with your mother – so beautiful; the yellow flowers on her dress, flat shoes and blonde hair fanning out as we danced across the bridge between the twin cities.

How I managed to come back here is no less than a miracle.

The let-go will take me home, home to my beloveds, home to real freedom, truth and love. My God! I sound like *you* did in 1968, so perhaps you will understand the taste I speak of. I remember that then I felt you to be foolish.

Now married, children, successful and comfortable twenty years on, the position is changed. I know you were right. Now you are just distracted from your nature.

That closeness you had then is more real for me now than is your own practice and breakfast on the terrace.

My love, I must soon leave, as I wander even now toward home. I see this time a future where the wandering is over, a silence in a nothingness ... no, not just nothing, a full nothingness. I heard of it in India, two words for nothing. One – Rikta. Just nothing, boundaries only. The other – Shunya. Pregnant nothingness, a full emptiness, bursting with every possibility. I know it's true, truer than the bedspread or the light playing through the window.

My love, tell the children and Jo that I go, not to what you will see – my body senile, old and dribbling. The middle distance that I stare into is full, my love, with truth.

I wander through my life until, when finally empty, I will find the light within all.

Beloved, I go home.

Goodbye,<br>Father.

# I CAN SEE WHY THEY CALL IT ECSTASY

*It's just here. All the time. Nowhere to go. Nothing needs doing. Well, almost nothing, sort of...*

*I* am not interested in contemporary drugs. They don't seem to bring out nice things in people, are made by some mad sod in a shed, and are mostly amphetamine-based. I don't need the aggravation of speed and impurities of rough -made drugs. Thanks, but no thanks.

I have an inherited daughter who did ecstasy for a short while when it was first available. She is young, so she did it in a dance scene. I was worried and looked it up online; then gave paternal advice about vitamin B and the like. She was pleased that I loved her and hugged me. She said, "This is a good drug, you should try it." I didn't.

She came later, saying that the drug had changed and she didn't like it anymore and wasn't going to take it again. I was pleased. My feeling on the matter is that drugs have been uncivilized since Sandoz stopped making acid.

When I visited Peter next I asked him about it. He had, of course, used some and agreed with Tara. "It was an astonishing drug, mate, not so good now as it has changed compounds. It still uses the same name, but before that it was very good indeed."

We talked more and I agreed that, if it were still as it was, I would be tempted.

About a year later he came to visit and I met him in the Botanic Gardens at midday to spend the afternoon raving and walking in a most beautiful place.

"Have you had lunch, mate?" I hadn't, and we had a light snack at a nearby Italian place. Sitting with glasses of water after eating, he produced two tablets from his pocket and said, "This will make you larger."

I trust him, so I took one and held it in my hand. Some things just ripple with power, and this was one of those. I felt that I held some key to pass over something. "What's this ,mate?"

"Ecstasy, old style. I got it from Sydney. A dear old mate had it and I tested it. It was true, and now we have the very last of it, one each in a beautiful place. Take it and come with me into the gardens."

I was hesitant, then suddenly stuck it in my mouth and took a drink. Can't get it out now, I thought.

"Well and bravely done, that soldier! Now drink the rest of the water."

I did. We had another glass at his insistence, then he paid the bill and we went outside. All was as before.

The lotus pond in the Botanic Gardens is one of my favourite places in the world. It was in blossom so we went straight there; it was, as always, quite beautiful. I was watching myself carefully. Peter said I should relax – it was all going to be fine soon enough. It didn't make any difference; I still watched.

We found a sign at the far edge of the pond that spoke of the lotus and its place in Eastern philosophical thought. At the end it said in parenthesis, "And Buddha sat thus." I was pleased with the imagery in the face of the flower's simple beauty and told Peter. He nodded agreement.

Two pale European tourists of middle age arrived, kind of white and pudgy and wearing the wrong clothes for the weather. I offered them the sunscreen in my bag and they accepted it gratefully. While they were applying it we chatted.

They had never seen lotus flowers blooming before. Weren't they beautiful? I said, "Yes, they are," and felt Peter's hand on my shoulder.

I looked toward the man who was thanking me for the sunscreen and he was alive with light and silence. I reached for the sunscreen and said, "You're welcome, mate." Not manners, I meant it.

As I took it from him I saw my hands; complete, I felt. Just hands, but endlessly silent and alive with all possibilities. I loved them. I build things, and they were absolute in their waiting coherence. No thinking, just seeing.

"Are you here too, mate?" I asked.

"Ah, yes" said Peter.

I heard the woman reading the sign and wondering out loud what "Buddha sat thus" meant. I said without saying ,"It's a bit like Harley Davidsons I think. If you have to ask, you won't get it." We laughed across the park together and I turned as Peter said to me, "You were always profound ,brother, you really were."

I looked into his face and saw that he meant it. I saw an ancient friend of aeons gone and the deepest of connections winding silently on and on forever. I smiled and hugged him. We went to the drinking fountain and he insisted I drink. I didn't mind, so I drank. I certainly wouldn't have thought of it without a reminder.

Looking was enough to take away all else. Nothing was different – not like acid that takes you somewhere – but here; this. That was all. I noticed a gap in my perceptions; names weren't there as I saw things.

I told Peter. He thought that was the key. No names unless called up, so no associations, no positive, no negative – just here, now. This leaves a space for bliss to come. We had heard it all before and this seemed to fit the bill very nicely.

He was right. Simple seeing of existence, nothing else

and the vast silence and joy of this existential experience was upon me. Nothing else was necessary. Good.

We walked. I saw a spot with water and fine plants. We sat a while and I would have continued to do so, but Peter said, "That's a big difference between us, mate. I can't sit in the silence. I have to move in it or why?" I said that I felt the silence and its nature was my essence too, what reason to move? Where to go to?

We agreed with each other and then walked. Why not? I thought. It made no difference; the landscape was still silent, still blissful and eternal, just moving. People came past, all friendly, looking the same as all things and us. I wondered aloud why people danced as a forum for this experience.

"I dunno, mate. They are younger, I think that is it."

I felt the power of youth unable to sit and pushed to move wildly, energy pulsing and coursing. They would have no choice, I thought, particularly with music and loving brothers and sisters near. There was no change, no meaning, so we spent a silent and beautiful afternoon together in the park.

Nothing was amiss, the world was as it was and therefore, as Buddha sat, as it should be. All was as it should be, and inside me I suspect it still is.

As we walked away from the drinking fountain again, totality ours, I remarked to Peter, "You know, this is not visible. If you weren't aware, there is no outside indication of the bliss inside. It simply is, and it just does not manifest."

"Well, sort of, mate. Except that you are holding my hand."

# HERE BE DRAGONS

*You can't rely on anything forever.*

As I walked through the front door into Max's place, I saw lots more space than before. Many things were missing. Max is not monastic; he has the proper amount of home base equipment. The kitchen table and chairs were gone, plants too; and the window sill was empty.

"Where's all your stuff gone, man?" I was lost as to why Max would purge his stuff. His answer was a surprise.

"I am moving up onto the river, mate. I am going to restore furniture for an antique shop and be there to sell it."

"Well, I'll be stuffed. How long for?"

I could tell it was for a while, as big furniture was going. Max took the kettle and filled it from the rainwater tap and put it on the stove. He turned to me and said, "Mate, I don't think I will come back. It's a nice tourist town in the wine area, and I should be okay. I'm fond of the river, too."

He scratched his knee through the hole in his jeans. "I like the sound of it and I always was good with the furniture."

I was staggered. If there were a chair I would have sat down. Old furniture was one of the things Max did – buying at auctions, spending time and skill with it, and selling it on. A little extra cash and a nice thing to do.

I was worried, so I asked him, "Will you keep this place on, mate, in case it doesn't work out?"

I felt like the Pope had just told me he was moving out of the Vatican. Max was getting teaspoons from the drawer.

"No, it'll work out in some way. I have been here a long time, you know. Anyway, it's like the bathtub. After you sit still a while you have to move or you can't feel the heat."

Such a lot of personal history in his place – many watershed moments and a sanctuary that I valued deeply, judging by how I felt on finding it was soon to vanish. I watched Max pour boiling water with great care into the teapot.

"Have you told Neil?" I wanted to talk later to someone else about it all. Max grinned. "I think everybody but you knows, mate. None of them believed it. They all looked like you do."

True. Get over it, I thought. Good on you, Max, for doing something. He poured the tea.

"You bastard! I fucking knew you didn't have a tea strainer." I was almost screaming. Max grinned again.

"I do. I just never use it. Special today only if you like for your shocked self, if you must. You're in the land of manly tea, mate, and it's really about time to get used to it."

I felt better at being held in loving contempt over a long period. It implied commitment. We went outside with the tea and sat on the old log. Max asked if I wanted to take over his house. I could have afforded it easily. It was one of those great hippie finds, solid and under-equipped, owned by an old man who didn't care to maintain it and charged a few dollars a week, just to be able to forget the place.

"Well, any other time, mate; but just now I am on the move too." I was, too, in the strangest way I could imagine.

"Oh, you keeping a secret are you, mate? Come on, out with it."

"Shit man, I haven't told anyone about this and I will be gone in a month. And for God knows how long." Max sipped and waited. I was almost embarrassed, it was such a weird, from the edge of the world type of story. Oh well, I thought, here we go.

"You know I am going to the States in a while to race the solar car?"

He nodded.

"I am going to leave early and meet a woman."

Max put his tea on the grass and leaned back. He was privy to the solar car episode. I was involved with a team from the local state school, constructing a race car using the collection of worn-out tools the government provided.

There was stunning community support from the small town around the school and a solar assisted vehicle was built. It had taken three years and the commitment of a lot of private time from lots of people. At the end of all this effort I had gone to the middle of Australia with the team and helped to win the race against comers from all over the world. We didn't mean to, really. We were just in the workshop giving bored kids a snappy thing to do.

After you win a world championship everybody wants to help. The Federal Government had funded the team and vehicle to the USA to race in something called the 'Solar Bike Rayce'. I was going. I planned to leave early and then fly to meet everyone at the race.

"You know I have a VW, Max."

I looked at him.

"Mate, you have always had a VW. Where are we going here?"

I sipped the tea – peppermint with honey. Nice.

"Well, I am on an email list. All over the world Van owners write and exchange bullshit ideas and complain about breaking down."

It was sort of true, except that we all loved our vans and looked after each other in terms of technical information; and felt like a family with a secret.

"Last year, early, there was a letter from a new person, wondering if she would ever get her new purchase running right as she saw only indications of unreliability on the list."

I stopped for a breath.

"Yours goes alright," Max interjected.

"That's what I told her, mate. They do, but not until you fix all the crap that the previous owner left undone because they knew Volksies would go forever without attention. Anyway, we started to chat back and forth online."

"Oh, man, you're having an Internet Romance! Wow – that's a trippy thing."

He was right. I had heard of it and seen pictures in the early days of marriages that started with internet communication of some sort. I always felt the whole thing was a bit dubious and for the socially ill-equipped. I told Max this.

"Not so. Such a mix of consciousness there. All in a new form. Impossible to predict what will happen and shouldn't yet be judged about how it connects people. I don't like it for music, but for digital communication I reckon it goes very well indeed. Go on, mate. I am all ears."

"Well, it was surprising how quick it all started to happen really. Lots of things dropped into place and, after a certain number, I sort of felt a tumbling and I was suddenly very involved indeed. Anyhow, the time zone is opposite so we were sending five or six emails a day and then getting all of them answered the next day. That was nice."

"That's a sort of compressed time, mate, that you are running six conversations at once, together, instead of one. Makes the time six times longer in exchange terms than it really is."

I liked that idea, as I now seemed to have taken a reasonable time to become besotted with someone I had never met. He asked what she was like. I told him about the common ground, the similarities in values, and how we both came from the same dead hippie planet.

"What does she look like?"

"No bloody idea really. She used to swim so she has shoulders. Says she looks okay so I suppose she does. She sounds nice on the phone."

His question worried me because I really did not care. I was in the love. Gone and beyond minding. Max breathed in and sighed, then stood carefully up and took the cups to make more tea and said, "Brave, the pair of you."

I followed him into the remains of the kitchen. I was not expecting to see it for a while after I went to the States, but 'never again' was tricky.

"Well, it crossed my mind that she might be the mouthpiece for a bunch of whatever the opposite of misogynists is and they would all come to the airport to point and laugh."

Max grinned, looked at me and said, "Then what?"

"I don't know. Buy them a drink and come back here to see you and find you gone, you miserable bastard."

Actually I hadn't thought in terms of failure at all.

"Well, bloody good luck to you, I say. Good to see we are all still crazy. How about it being in America?"

This had been an issue to me. I didn't know how I felt about the US of A and its ways in the world, as I never had to deal with it directly.

"Sort of still caught up in the old Vietnam opinions and wondering what it is really like there. You know, the subculture and value system we sit easiest in flowered there, and so did almost everything I fucking hate about the world, so buggered if I know really."

Max got his front door key. "Sounds like fun to me. Let's go out to the pub and eat a goodbye meal before we board ship. They will have a table there. And chairs too, if we are lucky."

# A WORD TO THE ENLIGHTENED

*I had an enjoyable exchange via email regarding enlightenment
with a couple I will call Paul and Kate, My wife, the
American, lost boundaries of self, as they had too, and we were
hoping to meet them. Paul is no longer with us and Kate has
not been in touch. I never asked permission to print their replies
to me so they're not here. It seems that people don't have to let
go of things to have enlightenment; things can let go of them.*

*H*ere are some extracts from my emails:

I don't know where to start of course; our Australian arrival plans are in disarray, for strange reasons. Trudy
doesn't mind my doing this in the hope we can meet, but I
am sure that left to her own devices she would not bother.
I remember how truly pleased she was when we ran into
Carole, the other empty, and enjoyed a meal. So I do bother.

Of your stories I know this: Kate awoke without self one
morning – whether the inner work and/or the LSD has any
relevance who knows? You were unwittingly poisoned into
it. A let-go of endless dimensions. I have ideas about physiology and consciousness, it seems you went via the physiology,
and Kate, through the consciousness.

Trudy's story: early days she spent years in meditation
with M. Yogi in Switzerland. Prior to that during high school
about 500 LSD experiences. I mention both these as I reckon
they all educate one to flow with events internal rather than
fight.

Also she was abused as a child, so her enculturation was a bit iffy. She married an abuser who physically hurt her and threatened her life consistently for many years. There were three children. When she finally left him, he extended abuse through wide-ranging and protracted litigation, finally taking the children from her and into an abusive environment.

During this process, the legal machinery destroyed every single support system she had. So after the children had gone she was alone in the house she had purchased with them in mind. She had noticed for awhile, even before the litigation, that she had no attachment other than the children and that they were now gone. After grief, isolation and depression for two years, she walked by the phone table one evening and said inside "I'm done, I quit" and let go. Remembers a peace and happiness and a silence inside:

*Like a falling open. It wasn't that I didn't recognise it as enlightened, I was not thinking like that anymore. Just: "Oh I've died, there is no-one here. No-one's home anymore". I didn't care, it didn't make any difference, it was just quiet and peaceful.*

She didn't recognise it at all as enlightenment. She had memories of the Maharishi saying that women can't be enlightened and when you are there are fireworks. It came from good karma which she obviously didn't have as she had lost the kids. It didn't fit the philosophy or teaching. It never left her. She spent the next three years pretty much alone and silent except for the fortnightly visits from the children.

I came on the scene online via a Volkswagen Van mailing list as her son had a van; we chatted via email and one day I rang her.

I have sensitivity to this state, I don't know why; Trudy says it seems I have been empty and lost it earlier. Maybe about early adolescence. It is possible as I don't remember the time well excepting a sort of annihilation from abusive parents coming to a peak and me sort of wandering inside for a time.

The moment she spoke, or really the moment she stopped speaking, I knew there was no-one in there. I asked about it, "Are you empty?" She said she resisted it as she felt her kids would sense her absence and be frightened. I should have been so parentally fortunate. I told her what I thought. Later I came to the USA, we got married and went honeymooning to Boulder to see Gangaji.

In Boulder we met Carole, the other empty in the sequence. Carole had gone to a 'relax American-style' event, entered into a guided meditation and awoke 'in hell'. Nothing real, everything flat, no God, no nothing. Also her eye began to tic. They were overjoyed to see each other and I organised us to go to dinner at the local Indian restaurant. We spent a few hours, they confirmed each other and we came home. We all exchanged details and completely failed to make contact again. I imagine she is in the American Midwest somewhere, quietly adding to the general effulgence of the world.

Carole  had come to Boulder and Gangaji because of something in Suzanne Segal's book *Collision with the Infinite*. Trudy was Suzanne Segal's best mate in TM, and they shared a home in San Francisco afterwards, while they both studied. Suzanne was claimed at a bus stop in Paris for heavens' sake.

It all reminds me of circular breathing on the didgeridoo: you work and work at it with exercises and effort; if and when you get it, it has nothing to do with the exercises, there's a let-go of trying. Still the exercises seem like they might have provoked it, maybe. If you see what I mean.

I read something by Rumi yesterday about being dragged to the garden in chains and not wanting to come. "Most of us here come in chains, very few came by themselves."

What a difficult email to write this has been, no proper

starting point and a fearful feeling not to muck it up etc. I hope it finds you both well and I am fully envious of everyone in the Australian countryside,

Yours Sincerely, RB

PS. Apparently my grammar and punctuation resemble an Indian train timetable in that they relate in no way to reality. My apologies and I hope you manage. RB

*Kate replied and was clear that she felt that the inner work the night before her emptiness was very relevant. She had known Maharishi in his earlier days in London and stated that at that time he had not indicated enlightenment as 'gender driven'.*

*She said that both she and Paul disagreed 'absolutely' with Rumi, as there was no garden and no one to go.*

Kate and Paul,

Slow reply from me as much is happening. I must say I pity the likes of Rumi as poetic souls trying to place words into the beyond as anything but the most distant of indicators. In the language of the Australia that I am missing deeply: buggered before you start!

Telling Trudy's story to you has evolved into a bit of an entertainment for me really. It began with my noting that we were attempting to be in Australia soon and necessarily spending a day in Sydney where I thought you were. We (she in particular) had enjoyed the company of an empty we met in Boulder, and I suggested trying to visit you, she said to go ahead and try to organise it and here we are. She is neither interested nor uninterested but doesn't mind and I am having fun. I am sure she would write if you wanted.

You ask good questions. Suzanne and Trudy were best mates in the TM movement in Switzerland and both spent years in the top end of the movement's hierarchy. She says she never heard directly from Maharishi that women couldn't be enlightened, but received it as a message on several occasions from 'his boys' after she could no longer speak with him directly. The reasoning was that the female physiology was too weak to maintain the experience. Both she and Suzanne left with similar observations to those in Suzanne's book. Incidentally, at the same time I did TM for a number of years in Oz and left it after doing the TM Siddhis programme.

Trudy came to San Francisco and isolated herself almost completely until Suzanne turned up and sort of pulled her into the world again. They shared a house for student years in SF. And then Suzanne left for Paris, Trudy is a psychologist also btw. One more reason I am doing this is that she is v. busy in the demanding American workplace.

The abuse thing dovetails into a lot of stuff for me. Trudy notes that every spiritual thing she ever had anything to do with had a large contingent of abuse victims. Why, I suppose, would those content with their lot seek a greater reality?

We don't subscribe to any inner self or suppressed personality seeking air as an idea for the basis of this experience either. This experience is not related to anything before of the personality or perception. Beyond means beyond and mysticism is not emptiness.

From here on these are my thoughts on the matter:

Now about LSD and abuse and Paul finding himself there etc. I see patterns as I go along in this. I remember M. Yogi and many others associating consciousness and physiology as one reflective entity. It seems so. I base the remainder on this premise.

Now I feel that this state cannot be 'achieved' in the normal sense. However I reckon it may be possible to provoke circumstantially.

Consciousness takes solid limited form as personality through social conditioning and the contractive response to sanction. I know how big that statement is. Please bear with me. The limiting mechanism seems to be the avoidance of again experiencing these and other incidental 'negative' past experiences, or experiences that parallel them and thus bring the contractive response. Behaviour is limited and order is maintained. A bit rough I know, but my typing is poor so I don't expand.

Given that it is physiology and this limited consciousness (or should I say 'personality') maintaining the integrity of the induced perceptual framework and that you two, for instance, have gone from it, there seems to be a precipitant with you both that dissolved the frame that relates to one of these two things (physiology or personality/perception).

In Trudy it was a personality/perception shift and when the frameworks were all proved untrue there was a moment of opportunity to not build somewhere else and simply be in the emptiness. She accepted it and there she isn't.

The body follows the shift of perception in this example. This I feel may take time and could be a bit rough.

Acceptance is why I mentioned the LSD. My memory of acid is that it was pointless to resist. Trudy wanted to be dipped in it. I feel that acid's main gift to us may be the capacity to

1.  Accept rapid changes in consciousness and the sudden appearance of the unlikely.

2.  Note that our regular state is not cast in stone as some eternal and absolutely correct pivot.

Similarly abuse gives one a mistrust of the world's ways, a deep and abiding knowledge that there is a base of lies in societal structure. This could lead to the non-stickiness of socialization in abused people. A similar result to acid.

Now, Paul seems to have had his physiology neutralised in his near-death expericnce, returning with none of the gifts that society has given us to filter and select our experiences and left only with a live empty physiology to reflect reality. The body changes in this example, the consciousness as personality/perception without effort returns to consciousness alone.

I think this can be true to varying degrees, the NDE people I have met have all, at least, returned with a sense of reality based in/adjusted by the emptiness even if they don't carry it experientially full time.

Kate seems to have come in through the other non-door of consciousness as personality/perception to return to consciousness alone and in that moment also accepted, and went the non-way of you both. The physiology would follow.

It happens; the mind can't do it or see it or in any way do anything to be that. This doesn't mean that it is not a process and until that last instant it seems sequential and logical, leading to a moment of opportunity. Kate's saying that her inner work of the night before is relevant, for instance, is a good example.

Critical here is the acceptance of the emptiness; one could recoil from it and become re-engaged. Sort of slip-out and stay there.

I reckon that here is the point where methods arise – not to enlighten one but to loosen one's enculturation so that when the moments come, acceptance of empty reality may too. This is the barest of bones and I will expand on any bit you like, but I sense not too far from some coherence. What do you reckon?

Hope this finds you both well,
RB


*There followed no reply. I suppose people track them down and they get sick of it, so it goes. Or maybe they didn't like the sound of me, hard to say. Kate was unwell and I hope that wasn't why she didn't reply.*

*I have noticed that all the enlightened people I ever met are different, having a sort of flavour from before. That is I guess why I feel easy with some and not others. Paul more than Kate. I loved Osho, such a mind and such a stirrer. However, there are others I don't like even though they are empty for sure.*

# A PEACE SIGN IN CALIFORNIA

*Being in the U.S. of A., and an old hippie, gave me the chance
for a pilgrimage to the home of the Grateful Dead. I did the
tourist thing and went to San Francisco, California, found the
Haight-Ashbury area. I liked it. It also made me think of home.*

*C*rossing the bridge in San Francisco, there was a guy on a
Harley; someone cut him off. He went past and twisted the
offender's rear vision mirror.

Just another city now. It wasn't always. In 1969 the place
sang a song that changed the world. I was going to see where
it all happened and check the remains for signs of life.

Off the bridge and after some industry, a nice old part of
town with the sort of inner city feel that comes from a long
time passing. As I walked I made mental notes.

Big parks and old gum trees. Lots of ancient eucalyptus
trees, maybe the biggest I have ever seen. Eucalyptus trees…
I felt homesick. America is the same size as Australia if you
include Alaska – and there are only 20 million people in
Australia. I missed the space of it; that you can be properly
alone, with nobody for miles.

I moved on. Little coffee shops, all with good food and
coffee. Tables with students on, and writing and reading. A
100-year-old dog. Groups of nerds talking about some new
application they are writing a review of. A Seinfeld look-
alike. All taken in as I sat with my nice salad. Good sort of
feeling.

Nice city streets, lots of overhead power wires and poles

just like I remembered from some Robert Crumb cartoon. I thought he just made it look like that, but it is real.

I went walking to find Ashbury, looking along it for Haight. At first the wrong way – a long way – and finally asked at a corner liquor store. All corners have 'likker' stores, each one run by some person looking middle-eastern. How are they treated since 9/11? I wondered.

As I moved toward the corner of Haight and Ashbury Streets, I was excited, really felt like some sort of pilgrim. There it was, a corner in a city... nobody there at all. I took a photo and went into the shop on the corner, a sort of a head shop but it was almost all shirts. I chatted to the guy, who told me he'd been 30+ years there and business was fine.

There were artefacts of sorts; stickers to display on your car, and mostly in that script I call 'Acid writing'. Mostly good. I bought a Grateful Dead T-shirt and spoke of them a while, of their integrity in the day and through the years.

The house they lived in was just up the road. Why not look? I remembered Phil Lesh speaking in front of it sometime on TV – good stories.

A couple of hundred yards up the hill there it was, 710 Ashbury Street, a nice little inner city house with a set of steps up. The gate post had "If my words did glow" and "Thank you Jerry" in black marker. I was blown away for some reason in that soft-feeling place, a centre of subcultural evolution. Felt like a power place that fills the senses and feeds the soul. Stronger than Sedona.

I took photos at the gate.

A 4WD drove into the attached garage, and the man driving smiled as he went in. As he came from the car to the front of the house with parcels, I asked, "Does all this drive you crazy?"

"No. Such nice kids most of them. It happens all the time."

I asked, "What happens?".

"They say, it's Jerry's place, and I say, no, it's mine now."

"They sound too young to have been Sixties kids," I say.

He went on. "We bought a couple of years after. It was empty and a real mess, lots of little cubbies and ruined bedding. We fixed it over the years and always there were people coming to see it. Outside, sitting, on the day he died there were a thousand there mourning I'm sure."

I marvelled at his patience. His own home a shrine for Deadheads and he had no affiliation; yet all he sees is nice kids.

At one time there were TV interviews on the house after Jerry had left, and he was sent tickets by the Dead to a concert. He said he loved it. So many people, having such a lot of fun, "and the music was nice too".

"I am jealous," I said, as I missed the concerts. He put the parcels on the car.

There was a Rumi calendar diary dog-eared under his arm. I pointed. "One of my favourite people," I said.

Conversation moved on, and we talked differently, all pleased and gentle in the world. He was a nice Krishamurti student – not the Krishnamurti who I felt doled out soft pap for consoling the half-hearted, but the other one who was directly and fiercely empty. We talked of Krishnamurti for a short while. He moved to go inside. I thanked him and reflected on the wonder of the symbols in front of me that day – from the extraordinary robust feel of the Dead house to the subtle extension of that high integrity bit of hippiedom movement – and suddenly it became a spirit spot with Krishnamurti who really knew that there is nothing.

I don't remember his name, but I know his heart, so sweet and kindly. Lone Ranger.

# BEFORE I FORGET

*I* went to the Third International Conference on Consciousness in Santa Fe in January 2003, with only one thing in mind. To see Isaac Shapiro. I had the impression that from him would come some key for me.

I was right; however, events conspired, as they do, and I drove the endlessly patient organiser on the other end of the phone to stretch point by cancelling, re-booking and then changing people numbers according to my own chaotic circumstance – several times – before even arriving.

It is as always under the circumstances. There is a part of me that can see and demands to be heard. I always go with it eventually, but without grace.

The catharsis and fear before I follow is difficult for all about me. There is never a mistake. When this feeling of "Go there. It is right" happens, it is not to be ignored. It is my deepest insight, a sleeping giant, waking when a signpost is needed. To where or to what end I am not certain, but growth in spirit so far. I have internally named this not-demon sleeping "Urge", after the less famous Kesey/Cassidy bus.

Finally, catharsis over, armed with one-day passes for Saturday (and one for someone that had decided not to come at the last minute), we arrived at the hotel at 2.00am on Saturday, having long been lost in old Santa Fe. We booked in and retired – all without the last minute person of course. I awoke to go to Isaac at 10.00am, all clean, properly attired and wondering why I'd bothered really.

It had started with his picture, you see. It seemed unpretentious and, well, ordinary. It woke up 'Urge' as soon as I saw it. Also, Isaac lives in Byron Bay on the east coast of Australia, and since I am Australian and was living in the USA as a matter of the heart, I felt sort of bonded.

We waited a while in the conference room as sound recording people fiddled about. All settled just in time. I saw Isaac as he came in – good, I thought. Corduroy trousers and a plaid shirt. A belly and a grin. He came in through the same door as we did, chatting to people as he went. Not an affectation in sight. I liked him out loud to my wife, who agreed.

It was immediately clear as he sat and welcomed us that he was the genuine article. Not because he fitted into preconceptions, just a silence ringing about us all.

I listened to the chat and followed as he led us as far as we would consciously go toward emptiness. Questions came and went, with Isaac gently using the experience of the questioner to drop them behind the question toward 'who was asking'.

I flowed easily with him, a kindly surgeon of consciousness. He went to the edge a number of times; that edge where ideas of perception are removed, the self, and experience is seen to be sensations. These sensations are filtered through our own ideas of good and bad experience, a sort of "do I want this?" moment, so that by the time we are aware of it, well, something else is already happening. Direct experience of reality thwarted by our own measuring devices.

With the carrying inside of not wanting an unpleasant event to be repeated and so watching for signs of its presence so we can avoid it, we are driven by that experience to shape our lives to the experiences of the past, and their avoidance in the present and future. A nice mess, really. And well put. I had heard it all before, but was enjoying Isaac's way with it, all enthusiastic and kindly to the people asking.

I was drifting with his words – a bit like they were sign-posts – and getting more and more silent. Nice.

People were asking to move toward practicality, politics and healing. I always felt that anything could be taken back to the pure consciousness that it came from; everybody holds different 'stuff' inside, so the path back is always different. Just as someone was getting sort of close to the edge, another person's question would come up. Ah, well, someone will drop someday, maybe.

I waited, listening to Isaac's reply to a question about shamanism, interesting uses of words, that the sacredness of something is lost as soon as it is described. Same as, he says. Words and concepts are not infinite, direct experience is. He said it again. The moment can't be described, as it is already gone. It is real as experience only; words take you from now into the mind.

All that is truly real is happening now. I surfed with it somehow, and stood inside self at the edge of a vast nothing. I had had this before and had always managed to come away. The fear of it was unbelievable; it smelt like insanity and death to me. I couldn't make myself come back properly and started to shake inside.

I must ask... oh shit, this is a trip. My hand was up in the air while other people kept asking things, and I was sink-ing into being terrified. I put my hand up and down as the conversation moved around, sometimes feeling okay and sometimes very not.

Suddenly the microphone was in front of me. Isaac was speaking, saying, (I have printed Isaac's words in italic, and me in plain text):

*What I was asking is, in your own experience is it possible to not have the experience that we're having? Look, even if you're dying or you're ill and you don't want that experience, what happens?*

*You still have it!*

*If you don't want it, what does the not wanting do? You miss it! You're in resistance to your own experience, but does the resistance help in any way?*

I got the microphone and with shaking voice say,

"I have quite a bit of trouble with this, Isaac. I've got no real difficulty with the momentary experience as an idea, but the idea is, of course, immediately separate. When I settle into this, what my mind response is, is just tremendous fear. It takes a moment..."

Isaac is onto it immediately.

*Beautiful! Oh, that is so beautiful!*

I don't know what I hoped for, but this surprised me.

"Isaac, I'm gonna cry, man! This is just too hard for me."

*Whats it's doing is it's pushing you right into...*

"Kid you not, it's pushing."

I feel insanity here, a madness without end.

*It's inviting you. You are here because something pulled you to be here?*

"Yes, I was pretty choiceless about coming to see you."

Really. I had cancelled twice, hassled the organizers far too much and nearly turned away driving here.

*That's what's interesting to explore: when we start to see that there's no possibility to not be in the experience that we're having.*

"Yes, but that's the very front of the train, and everything else that I add to it after that seems to me to be a falsity. You know, does it all have to go? I mean, every last bit?"

God, I hope not. Every last bit. I joke, it might help.

"Geez...I hate you. You empties are all the same you know."

Everybody laughs. I want it to stop and I don't sense mercy coming.

"It's huge and I'm just scared to death. I get right on the edge here... and I'm gone."

*So that fear is here right now?*

"Yeah."

*Great! For the first time now, just so gently, be in it. Instead of running away from it, just gently drop in.*

"That's a *big* ask..."

*Yes, it is a big ask, but what are the possibilities?*

I don't know, I will be insane it looks like.

"I ..."

*It's here. So just take a moment. It is here.*
    *Drop in. Just drop in. See what's in the middle of it, in the*

*core of it.*

I know what waits...

"Isaac, there's nothing in the middle."

Oh shit! I am going mad, falling and freaking. Oh shit! I hear Isaac say:

*There's nothing in the middle of it. Good. And now drop into that nothingness; BE that nothingness.*

What the fuck.. I went, shuddering and breathing deep and shaking, I went. Nothing, just nothing. A long time went. I came to and asked, "So... so now what?"

All quiet, voice too, but shaky in the speaking.

*Good! Just keep dropping. There's no mistake, you're here. What I can tell you is everybody that's ever woken up has been through this exact story.*

*So now, you're just being here, present in this nothingness. You're here. Some people call it like an abyss, or falling, or black hole – doesn't much matter. You're right here. And you're still here, right?*

"Yes."

I am frightened again.

*Good! So nothing bad is happening.*

"So far..."

*Just keep dropping into it.*

I don't want to be in the crowd, just to sit near Isaac. If he is doing this I want closeness. Or something. Just not nothing.

"Can I come a little closer?"

*Please do.*

I stand up and a sort of going happens, then there I am at the front, he is just there. I am frightened again.

*Please, take a seat. Good to see you!*
  *You're here and there's experience; and that experience now, as you spoke, was of nothing. Yes?*

"Yes."

*Good. Can you keep holding the microphone?*

I have the microphone in hand but it's dangling between my legs as I sit. I want to tell him of the fear.

"My response to it, as it goes, is horror."

*Horror: good!*

Horror. And more of the same. Without end.

*So now just drop into that horror.*

O God, I knew that, I just want it to be easier. This is a hell; I am not relaxed with it at all. The fear is back and it means business.

"Terrific – my favourite experience."

*You're here.*

As he talks I go, gently attend to the fear, my chest is torn and it all drifts – drifts like soft snow.

*You're still here; all that you're doing actually, if you can call it a doing, is a gentle exploration of what's been here always. At the core. So you're just gently exploring. From the inside. Just being in it, checking it out.*

Leaving nothing. Open-eyed nothing. Seeing and no response. Like an eggshell with eyes.

"This is different!"

My voice.

*What's happening?*

"Nothing!"

*Nothing? How is it?*

"It's alright ......"

God. It is kind, endlessly kind.

It is alright.

I feel cheeky, the sense of what has begun is there, and I want to laugh.

"...a bit boring."

*Good. Then drop through that boring.*

Oh. That is all, isn't it. Nothing – and as stuff comes there is attention and then there's nothing again. Isaac is laughing.

*What happens to the boring as you're in it?*

"Just a bit bubbly, you know."

*A bit bubbly? So we've gone from terror, to horror, to nothing, to boring, to bubbly – and really we're just sitting here. Just watching.*
*There's not much doing. We're not trying to change, or fix, or get rid of. There's just a being present.*

Mind has come back at bit; patterns are seen and words heard.

"Anything but *This* is an affectation."

*Anything but this is an affectation. If you could hold the mike up...*

"I'm sorry."

Oh, look, manners!

*That's okay. I know as you're losing your mind it's hard to keep it together.*
Super truth, I feel; still cheekiness comes.

"Bit tricky, you know."

People are not chatty now, they break silence with sudden laughing. I look and they are just there. No more, just there. As they should be really.

"I quite like this. It's... it's..."

*Now drop through the liking, even.*

I want some form here! But no, I either mean it or, I don't. So I go. Drop through!

People are laughing. I talk. Form. Please!

"There's a bus called Further, you know. It's like that, isn't it? Just further..."

I've read Jed McKenna you see, and in the Sixties I loved the Ken Kesey and the Merry Prankster buses most of all. So I will keep them.

*No, no. Just keep playing and exploring because what's opened up is actually exquisite. Most people spend a lifetime of searching to come to this moment, so I don't want to underestimate the profundity of what's happening right here. This is* awesome.
*Just keep exploring. I just don't want to stop right here. Drop underneath even the liking it.*

"It's just back to nothing again."

Real quiet now.
Nothing...

"Over and over again..."

*Open into the nothingness. Just open into the nothingness.*

"And it comes back to thought and affectation almost immediately."

*Okay. Good.*

"If you stay there it goes back to nothing again."

*So it seems to cycle at the moment. So you just keep exploring – just watching the cycling and just dropping underneath.*

I can't stop shaking. My chest feels as though it is physically tearing. And all in a wonderful silence.

"My body's responding really a lot..."

*That's fantastic. Of course, there's a total connection – except we can't even say connection – between body and mind. They're the same thing. We have words and we tend to organise all this into a mind and a body; but like I was saying, there's no separation between mind and body. So your body is, of course, having an experience.*

I get it. All of the books. Years of effort, everything, doesn't relate to this at all.

"If this is it, there's a lot of bullshit written about it, isn't there?"

Lots of laughter, but I meant it, not a joke.

"You know? I mean, there doesn't seem to be anything happening in here."

*Nothing happening in here. Good. So there's not much happening – except everything, except this. How is it right here?*

"It's pretty quiet, really. And I don't mind. My chest is ripping but I'm alright."

*Yes, you are alright.*

"There's nothing happening here. This is the first time I've actually liked this. This is alright and... it's a bit familiar."

*It is familiar. That's what's so awesome. You know, we wake up and realize we've always known this.*

"I think it's just ordinary."

*It's ordinary.*

"Will it stick?"

Isaac laughs.

*It's your nature. How could it not? You know – will it stick? Basically, what you're experiencing is yourself.*

Gratefulness comes.

"Yeah, well... thanks very much!"

Everyone laughs. I meant it, what else to say?

# THE WORLD WENT RIGHT ON WITHOUT ME

*But I got the steak knives.*

*I*t appears there is more to say:

"I have a very close friend who's an empty. You know, if you say 'enlightened' people can get a bit funny and she endlessly cops it from the world – and it really hurts. I'm not really looking forward to it if that's what's going on at the end of this."

*Well, what we call 'copping it' just gives us these opportunities to watch where there's an automatic resistance. The bottom line is, if we take the ultimate experience – dying – when you're not resisting dying, then it's beautiful.*

*What will likely happen in this, is the automatic habits to try and get away from experience will start to reveal themselves. When you notice where your system is in resistance to your experience, you'll see that there's so much energy tied up in the resistance because it's impossible not to have the experience. But whenever you recognise one of those ways in which your whole system is organised to avoid experience, so much energy is liberated. The energy is then available for being. That makes you even more sensitive and you see even deeper into the patterns and so it goes on. Every one of those habits makes it seem like there's a you there, or that it's personal; I can tell you that none of it's personal. It's just this beautiful process and consciousness...*

From nowhere, I say,

"What's all the fuss about then?"

*Then there's no fuss.*

"Sorry, mate..."

More manners.

*There's no fuss. So copping it always has to do with not wanting. Now let's just look at something. The moment you don't want to have an experience, all that happens is you have the experience and, on top of it, you have the experience of trying to do the impossible, which just makes it worse. And you're still having the experience! Except now more intense. And then you don't want that because now it's worse. So within a very quick few moments it's suddenly overwhelming, it's bigger than you, and you feel totally helpless, incapable of doing anything about it. So any time in your life that there's something going on that you don't want to be happening, just look at what happens inside of you. You're left with this feeling of powerlessness, hopelessness... Isn't it?*

Oh, a question; best tell the truth.

"I've no idea what's going on any more ..."

*That's okay. So for you, all there is at this moment is that you're just here – life is moving through you. Don't try and grasp anything with your mind. It's pointless.*

"I have to say this is *nothing* like expectation. You know, this goes alright, doesn't it?"

Isaac laughs.

*Yeah... so now I promised we'd come back to living the practicality of this.*

"Okay...can I stay here?"

*Please. Feel free.*
    *There are some important distinctions that happen as this waking up goes on; and one of those distinctions is to notice. For instance, if a car's coming towards you at 90 miles an hour, not to jump out of the way would be absurd. But you know, we don't actually have to think about it. Our bodies just move or they don't. So most of what goes on in our life is just...is just a happening.*
    *Here's a horrible graphic example I use: if you see a pile of steaming dog poop on the pavement, will you step into it? Chances are not, if you'd stepped into it even once before and you'd had the trouble of getting your foot out of it. If you don't see it it's just luck whether your foot's going there or not. So either way, there's not much choice. Once you see it, not much choice. If you don't see it, not much choice.*
    *So it's like this: our functioning in life goes on and if we don't see what's happening we just repeat the same stuff again and again and again and again. If we do see it and we start to see it in a way that's clear to us, it's over.*
    *So now, on a purely practical level in our lives, I was speaking earlier about contraction, tightening up. Then about this thing of moving from a place in yourself of overflow – or from joy – a movement in your life that's just sweetness moving. And that's what we're exploring here. Because ultimately, what we love the most is to move as love, to move as that sweetness.*
    *Anyone disagree with that? I mean, ultimately that's what it's about.*

*Our nature is consciousness and the direct experience of consciousness is nothing, but what that nothingness opens into is everythingness, which is love. And bottom line, what we love is to love. We love just to be true to our nature. Everything that we want to change or fix is because what we want at the core, is this feeling of love, this knowing of love.*

*But the difficulty is when we try and fix it and change it out there to get it in here.*

*Let's just look at this – if my happiness is dependent on how you're being, it means I'm a victim of how you are. This means the only way I can be happy is if I get you to be how I think you should be. Now to live in that paradigm, or that way, I found a hard go; because the only way I can be happy, basically, is if I get everybody else to be different than who they are. So it doesn't really work that well.*

*And we can see it in relationships. When we want our partners to be different, or our kids to be different, or our parents to be different – what happens inside of us? The bottom line is that we're making our happiness dependent on how other people are. We're out of depth.*

*We become a victim in our own way of functioning. And who do we ascribe our discomfort to? How they're being. So then the only way that we can be happy is by trying to control and manipulate and change 'out there'.*

*This way of functioning doesn't actually work for me to live as what I love; it works for me to live as, so to speak, a victim within my own consciousness.*

*Let's just explore this – has it worked for anybody here yet? Does anyone here know anybody that it's worked for in any country, anywhere, in any dimension? It doesn't work! Is that true? Is it safe to say that? Is it useful to see that?*

*If we don't see it, you could say we're already programmed to live that way. If we don't see it, we'll just keep doing it. If we do see it, it's like the dog poop. Once you see it, you don't have* to step into it. Or if you find you've stepped into it, you recognise – *"wait a second!"*

"Is George Bush a part of us?"

*Is George Bush a part of us, is the question. It's not even a part, you see. This is our thinking again. We think in terms like "you're a part of me", but when I start really looking deeply at that question... What is you? What is me, for that matter?*

*Let's start with me. What is me? And by me, I mean ask yourself that question. What is me? Just really explore that for a moment in your own consciousness, in yourself. Right here, right now.*

*First of all, are you your body? For a lot of people this is a tricky one. I am my body, I'm not my body. But, are you your body? No.*

*Your body's changing every moment. And what we can see is, if you look at your hand, you'll see that you're aware of your hand. Right? If your hands move, you'll see that you're still there. Anything you're aware of is an object to you, so you're not your body.*

*Are you your thoughts?*

*Your thoughts keep coming and going. Do you? Your thoughts are objects to you; they're something you're aware of.*

The shaman woman, speaking from the seats, says: "Yes. I am my thoughts, but I do come and go. I am not just here in this reality. I'm in other realities at the same time."

*Any reality that you experience is an object to you. You're the subject.*

"Yes..."

*You are that which is aware.*

"Yes..."

*And that awareness is not something; it's not an object.*

"No, it's not a physical object."

*It's not a physical object, and it's something you cannot describe, just like we discussed. You cannot describe it. Anything that you're aware of is an object to you.*

*I want to just loop round and come back to this George Bush thing. Clearly in our lives there is action, and that action happens. We like to think that we're the doer, but if you look in your own lives, the interests that have happened for you. Did you wake up in the morning and say, "Today I'm going to get interested in something"? Or did it just happen?*

"I'm a planner, so I'd have to say I planned it."

*You planned your interests?*

"In small steps."

*Yeah...Oohhh...*

Laughing ripples around.

*Honestly, do we plan our interests? They just happen. Isn't it? And we find ourselves moving in our lives. So these interests happen, by themselves. Do we plan? Look, can you say "Today I'm going to fall in love"? You can? Okay. Try it! It isn't how life actually happens. In our thinking, maybe.*

"That's my thought. I think "I'm going to fall in love today', and I believe, yes, if I want to, I will fall in love today. That's how strong I believe in my thoughts."

*I understand. But is that your experience? Is that the way it actually works? Look – right now – right now – get interested in nuclear physics.*

"I am."

*Okay. What are you not interested in? Motor mechanics, are you interested in that?*

"Yes, I am."

*Great. What are you NOT interested in?*

"Not interested in talking about ....knitting."

*Okay. Get interested; get interested in knitting then...right now. A passionate interest.*

"Okay. My friends would need..."

*Okay. But you can see that, if you try to do it by will, it's not something that's going to last very long at all.*

"I ....."

Isaac interrupts:

*Sorry, I have to wrap up. There's one more talk and we can just carry on then if you're interested and it's not in conflict with another thing.*

*So what we can notice is that, yes, there's an interest that's happened in you in wanting to be in this world in a way that's of service to the world, otherwise there wouldn't be an interest in working politically, or whatever. That's what the root of the interest is, and all we're doing now is just looking at that interest and refining it, to see that it can be an actual expression of being alive. It doesn't mean that the interest has to go; it's just refining how you are in your interests, whether it's in a way that's contracted or whether it's an expression of what we love the most. That you can explore.*

*That's the invitation.*

*Thank you for showing up.*

People like it, they clap a long time.

I thank him and go to lunch.

# FURTHER

*My mother always said that I would come to nothing.*

$I$ saw Isaac the next day. He said, "Things will start to happen pretty quickly now."

I was silent and seeing equanimity from somewhere behind my eyes. Okay, I felt, it will all sit on this screen and move past, no worries.

I wish. Life as a drunk lunatic driving a rollercoaster in a hurricane, merciless and without respite.

This place is not as thinking would have it. Not a place at all, but we speak, so we must limit. Imagine silence and emptiness, all bliss and integrated holistic experience. Well, I did too.

Forget it. It all has to go. Including the consoling day-dream.

Some collusion to believe between my body and mind has been broken, and my leading edge is now experiential, not mental. So, as if one end of a tension is broken and empty, the other end lashes. All to do is watch, and watch again, as the maddened gifts of conditioning and choosing and world form flay around a place that once had the affectation of walls to give them safety.

All is uprooted. Try to hold something: forget it. It will turn into a wisp of un-smoke as soon as you look at it.

Travelling along the edge of the Salt River Canyon in Arizona, looking over, the body filled with the ancient fear of heights I have always carried, a glance and it vanished, leaving the canyon alone, no emotion, nothing. Except the experience. Sounds good, fears leaving. Opinions too. And the endless chatter in my head, gone. But...

When I reached the White Mountains, all snow and cold, a nice big fire, and an armchair. Sitting among the warmth of old comforts and the many wood fires loved in my life gently flickering about me.

Guess what? Focus on the experience, it disappears, leaving nothing. Just a fire. Oh, fuck. Then, at a glance, even 'oh fuck' vanishes.

Empty means empty. There is no balm in Gilead. Reality? All done with smoke and mirrors. And, it doesn't like being found out.

As Isaac said, it *all* has to go, every last bit.

At this point, you wouldn't wish it on a brown dog.

Still, wait and see.

# THE MAD BASTARD'S GUIDE TO ENLIGHTENMENT

# WORDS

*C*ongratulations on getting past the title. The contradiction in words is an important thing to see. And disregard.

I don't like words all that much in this arena. They bring visitors. Enlightenment, for instance, is a bit like the pied piper. Thousands of children following. So I won't use it again. Awake will do instead; less preconceptions of appearance and behaviour, location or anything else.

I would have to say, if you asked, that it has always been like this. Although I know that I can point to a time, place and apparent person that something appeared to have happened to.

It is impossible to speak on this and be clear; it is beyond words, more the thing that words arise from, the thing that experiences words. Thing? No, it isn't.

But the truth is, it has always been like this. For you too. Everyone looks already awake, so some small mistake is being made, it seems, in the name of going somewhere more comfortable or holy. I see trying and effort, physiological purifying efforts, ritual, calming techniques, witnessing, soul-mating, all the stuff, and every last bit of it is playing on endless consciousness, already awake, already home. There is no-thing outside. Beyond means beyond. Infinite is not something that excludes anything. That's right – nothing is excluded, nothing is outside.

Now don't forget that for the time being.

Words and ideas are not the enemy here, there isn't one, there isn't a path or a destination, and you are already done.

You exist as you are and have the experience you have. Neither acceptance nor denial will help or hinder. Do you notice a Whitmanesqe style of contradiction here yet? Well, really, the moment this is subject to explanation, you're fucked really. It doesn't go there.

Most people seem to live in a world of descriptions, directly experiencing the world, and then in less than a nanosecond whatever is being experienced has a name. There ends direct experience.

The name serves to separate this experience from self, enabling all sorts of stuff to happen. As soon as the name is in place, a set of ideas arise and then there is a story, for instance; I fell from height when young. The experience called height and edge brought the story of injury and fear forever. These arrangements exist in us all. Stored neatly in physiology as memory and body responses. They occur with appropriate 'external' stimulus and some attempt to re-arrange reality follows. A recipe for total misery: "I will be fine if the world changes."

What problem is there in this? None really, all is inside consciousness, all part of the infinite play, but the moment is missed. Instead, the story lives as 'you' and you seem obscured by the story, grown from a description – and the joy of this very moment is obscured. Although what is not okay about the experience of a story? It *is* okay. It is perfect. If one doesn't freak out and seek happiness through trying to rearrange the real. Keep it if you want. Give the book back. Have a cup of tea.

Best advice ever. Give up.

Because, when this moment is not accepted for what it is (Stop! Don't go off and try to accept – that's bullshit), then you have judged from the past and purchased the ideas of better in the future.

What happened to now? All gone via conditioning, ideas

and physiology. This particularly includes the ideas around the E word we are not saying anymore. But this silliness stands firmly on language. Our labels. Look in the dictionary, our experience of the world is made of its contents. In the beginning was the word indeed. The beginning of illusion.

What to do? There isn't anything to do. It is already perfect, it is what it is, and the rest is a story.

Even the story is not a problem, Buddhas trying to be Buddhas is as much real as anything else is; it's all in the non-box. But it is a story. With boundaries. And when the focus is there, the boundless is not seen.

# WHAT'S IT LIKE?

*I*t's not like anything. Sadly, sounding like everyone else that speaks on this, I go on. I will say some stuff.

It's quiet. No more dialogue chatters in the mind, all vanished. It seemed like bullshit if I focus on 'before', but it stopped. In a nanosecond. Less.

It doesn't inform behaviour. Yes, that's right, it does not inform behaviour. More a sort of non-influence really, a noticing that certain doings, based on stories, are pointless, so they don't happen. This not happening is noticed in retrospect, mostly by other people. Everything is visually the same, seeing the same things everywhere as always, and there it is, just is. This gives a sort of non-motivation status really. Not that I don't do things, more that they get done, by nobody. Ambition, ha! I see typing now, for instance; it happens and that's all. Nobody in here in the terms that I vaguely remember defining self.

Memory is shot. Buggered beyond belief. Going shopping requires a list or supermarket-ness is happening. No idea what for, even the what for is not there. Linear simply doesn't function in a regular way. Everything gets done it seems, but just done, by nobody.

There is the centre of it really. Nobody is in here. That is the reality. Mind, physiology and language used to collude, and throw an illusory story of self on the screen of consciousness, but not now. Consciousness couldn't give a fuck of course, it is there for anything, and these other three have an internal agreement that there is reality in their dance. So a sort of stuckness appears to be happening. Like a feedback loop.

I sleep like a log. I always did, but now, when I close my eyes, I see nothing. Like a pregnant golden blackness. Waking up is like the world switching on all in a flash. There it is. It isn't, and then it is.

I am still doing the same stuff. Because, well, things happen. Not really, but I still do the same work and have the same car, clothes and like that. Because I know them. There is nothing, the old self is no more. When the world knocks on my door, the form instantly goes on like an old T-shirt. Convenient. The form lacks the meat on the bone it had, but keeps the world easy, so it stays, all by itself. "You're the same, but different." Yep.

It has a quality. Sort of. I hear of universal love and lots of other beaut words, but my experience is of a complete and endless kindness about it somewhere. Not with manners, but silently gently kind, that's all.

Apparently you can see it. To me that means it is familiar in you, recognition of your own emptiness. Nice.

Kids like it. Especially babies.

It is familiar. Like a dear old friend.

# WHAT SHOULD I DO?

*W*ho? Nobody there to do anything. Nowhere to do it. No-one to do it to. Or with. To go where? For what?

In this sense the whole pursuit will drive you nuts. So don't do anything. This experience is just that, experience. Not for the mind, it can't have it. Not that mind is the problem; the mind is what it is, the rest is a story. The body too, so yoga is hopeless as a technique of arrival, as there is nowhere to go. It functions well if you want a nice gentle exercise regime.

So relax. Have more tea, walk, whatever. It won't make any difference, do what you like.

I got talked into it. Words inside like a splinter, and other words like the needle to slip it out. Then both are unnecessary. If you like, go find someone awake and talk. That seems nice. Just keep mucking around with it, sometime you will get it. The tiniest shift. It is there already. In between, sort of. But not like that at all.

You will see, it can't be told, it isn't separate; where else can it possibly be, but right here. Now. (Stop trying to be here now.) It happens by itself. Trying is a story that says you are separate and that is obvious crap. Easy isn't it? Has anyone said nihilism yet? Another word. Go write a book with it.

There are times that it seems easier to re-focus. Null times, crisis times. If you find yourself driving, sliding sideways toward a tree, the mind is fucked. It simply stops. The body does what it does and there it is – direct experience.

Sink gently into it like a nice bath when it happens. Not with effort, just gravity... I can't tell you how everywhere it is. How obvious. How, well, omni-everything really.

I don't imagine mind likes hearing this at all, no edges, no descriptor, no box it fits in, and it has got to smell like death. It isn't, but the mind is thick, so it imagines bullshit. It is in the job specifications.

The world provokes this experience often; it is made of it utterly, so it must be so. This moment is a treasure, the only thing that is, so it waits to be seen, to welcome home the thing that is looking.

# MEDITATION?

*L*ots of people do something of the sort. Some for reasons of coping and some to gain quiet. Then there are those who see a direct path to awakening with meditation as a process of continuous refinement of thought and physiology, until finally, later, some bridge to the beyond opens and there they are.

I know a good few awake people now, and none of them would hesitate to say that this experience has no linear connection to anything else.

Including meditation. I met a woman recently who had the misfortune to wake up while doing a meditation course of some sort. She has a few people following her, as if she is going somewhere, and tells them that the only thing to do is to meditate endlessly and wait. To me this is total bullshit and thank God she didn't wake up in the spa, or there would be these poor wrinkled sods waiting wetly for the skies to open for them. There seems to be a logic in it. But I meditated in one form or another for years, it did not bring awake one tiny bit closer. And it won't.

With that in place, the experience of meditation itself is strangely similar to awake in a distant way. Some objectivity, some connectedness, quiet, silence even. The difference is that the awake experience has no centre, none. A decent meditation gives something similar, but with a false centre. Like watching the breath, witnessing, or using a mantra, not uncommon forms of meditation. The old self watches breath or gently mumbles like Patanjali said, all other experience gravitates toward what seems normal to me. But the mind is now being trained to watch as an observer and the experience that is watched becomes the observed. Then we have cleverly trained one bit of the mind to watch another. Too messy for me.

Its only possible function seems to have experience that enables you, should you awake, to not fear it, or to accept it as familiar in some way. Well, it is familiar anyway, it is all that is. You never left. So there is little point to meditation in awake terms. Except to perhaps lessen the shock to the body should grace take you.

A number of people now gone to silence used LSD a lot, I mean a lot. The common thing for them seems an easy acceptance of the awake focus, from the acid training, that it is futile to resist rapid consciousness change, so they relaxed into the experience as it happened. A gift, but expensive wrapping. I wouldn't bother with that either, like there is somewhere to go again.

# THE BODY?

*L*ook after it. The thing that is looking lives nearby, reflects in and out of it, and it is a bit of a shock to the body, this waking up. Not too much, but if you are gently fitter it certainly appears less bother. It is also where the physical bit of the story lives, and if it loosens, then it is more a comfortable time if the body is fit, so why not?

Please remember physiology is not relevant to waking up at all, consciousness is as clean in everyone's body, whatever. Really this is about comfort and ease. After waking, the body doesn't hold the storage of past at all well and the changes are real and can be felt. Anything stored from the past with attention on it will come up to have satsang, and will be felt in the body. That includes the attention that says no; the looking to choose the positive has attention on what to avoid, so they are both present and equal. These are all arranged and neatly balanced, look to the mind like a person. Which brings me to a bit of a thing:

The meditations that I did for an eon were no use at all in waking up; are now as relevant as the tyres I choose for my car.

But, after waking, as things moved in the body, the capacity to just see, without acceptance or denial, looking only at the sensations passing, seems easy, and that could be because body is familiar with simply allowing experience as used to happen in meditations. So maybe meditation is useful in making the not-road to nowhere on which no-one travels to nowhere else smoother. But not as a vehicle or a science of arrival.

Remember, the experience of life goes like this: 'external trigger' from outside events, naming, and the 'internal response' from the body. Then the story comes, like the falling event, and the fear that stays with you afterwards. After waking, the story is gone, the body will still, as always, be present to outside events. With no story reinforcement the body is free to relax. And it does.

Isaac Shapiro, who was the wordsmith at waking time, said immediately after, "Things will start happening fairly quickly now..." It is true, tumbling endlessly and things going past like shapes in an endless silent flowing, visiting as the senses bring reminders. Things, old things, that had substance, but no more, the silence sees them and they relax into that silence that sees. The hold in the body that helped limit experience will relax into vastness.

Such a roller-coaster filled with lively gasping nothings. I wouldn't be dead for quids.

# WHERE IS THE MIND IN THIS?

$S$ame place as everything else. Nowhere. It sort of seemed to be the driver before, giving a sense of self and seeking to evaluate everything. All that simply vanished in a moment. Layers and layers of the most refined storytelling, giving a centre that seemed so solid. It comes and goes. Usually quickly.

Life moves by itself and seeing happens – to nobody, remember. The mind pretends to be boss, well, because it has no other function. Living life with the mind acting as if it is in charge is like continuously knowing you must drive important nails in, so you carry a hammer in hand always.

After awake, it is self-evident that the nails were imagined and no hammer is necessary or real. Even if nail happened, it would be self-driving, or a hammer would be picked up and driving would happen without pretending, or self, to nobody. Like that.

It isn't for explanation; there is no reference point. All this is just wording it around until mind gets fed up and stops really. It isn't important. Or useful in this matter. Not a bit. Don't take notes.

Drink more tea. Walk. Talk rot with your mates. Watch cricket. Have your hair done. Scratch yourself. Or not. But you cannot think your way to awake. Not even one tiny bit. Wanting it is a pain in the arse too. It is not science; it is not even art; more just a trick.

# THEN WHAT'S THE DIFFERENCE?

*A*h. Seems like a great question. And with the information we get from the awakened it is. There is no difference. None. Everything is the same. All the cups are on their hooks, the car is in the garage and so on and on. Everything in its place. It is how it is.

Now if the last sentences read, "and so on and on. Everything in its perfect place. It is how it is."

*Perfect* place is what's different. Not as a belief in a great order of God, or a karmic wheel in balance; these are ideas, thoughts. They exist to hold up the judgement of their opposite. Perfect placement is because I no longer see the cups and then think of any story to go with them. More simply, cups are seen. Nothing. Just there. No opinion. Now if body wanted a cup of tea and opened the cupboard door then cup will happen. And tea will simply be made.

This will be said, to you who are earnestly seeking mindlessness with the mind, a million times and a million ways. There is no point in trying to work this out. It is its own boss. It is all there is and it happens everywhere all the time. No question about it. It is presence itself, underscoring everything. *You* trying to be present so you can experience it, no. Awakening happens and then presence is just there. No *you*.

It is truly a reading nightmare. It's a circular pile of words. And the mind will say now and then, "I get it!" But it is lying. There, now, sits all things as they were, as they should be, and are. Nothing else happening. To nobody. Like your house, when you leave. Like the cups when you are not looking. Things go on. To nobody.

There was a sort of real difference, in the body. For awhile. It seemed slower to completely respond to the experience of emptiness than the other components of experience. All the conditioned responses are stored there, they don't go anywhere. But in the presence of awakening they sit with no collusion from the mind to empower them and I imagine feel quite useless. Certainly as they arrive they look silly. Not being responded to and fed they relax. More and more. Then the input that triggered its response doesn't so much. Less and less. It isn't a difference really. Just something happening now. But it isn't important.

And the opposite doesn't apply, just in case yoga was looking like a path for a moment there. Awake and mind/physiology are not linear in both directions. It is a relationship called intransitive. Because awake relaxes the body, doesn't mean relaxing the body will awaken you. It's nice to do and it may be useful if the awakening accident happens, but not connected.

# I HAVE A GURU

*I* always want to say, when I hear this, "I have a Mitsubishi." But that, while true, isn't helpful.

The guru thing is so tricky, I look back and see people in guru positions in the world who were so kind to me, so loving and special. I am grateful for their presence in the world then, and when I see them now I am always glad.

But when I woke up, it wasn't them. It was me. I saw. It happened, and the veil fell.

For all my gratefulness for the kindness, I look now and see that I might as well have been at the beach looking. Or anywhere else. It was a quiet and meditative time, gentle in so many ways. But it is no more or less awake than anything else. There is no path toward or away. No method, no science of awareness to assist.

Having said that, it did make the mind quieter and life is nicer with less noise. Also surrounded by quieter minds was easier than the opposite.

So as a thing to be doing I have not the slightest criticism or opinion. But if you expect to sit before someone and have them give it, or bring you even one bit closer, it is a fool's errand. It is more digital than analogue. A yes/no function. It happens when it happens, a happy accident. And it decides.

Awake gurus expose you to presence they carry, that's nice. It is like a reminder letter, but you pay your own bill. I have no advice on the matter of guru, or Mitsubishi, that is useful in a person's awakening. I liked it some, and I liked cricket and tea too. Still do. None of it is separated from the thing that looks.

If you want to, do it. If not, don't bother. It doesn't matter one whit. Infinite is inclusive. Perfect.

# NEW AGE MOVEMENTS

*I* am staying with a friend, there is a gardener who came in for a break and asked for help with the coffee machine, I said I would and started to turn the familiar switches; she said "You're a Scorpio aren't you?"

It must be clear to anyone who looks, that the world doesn't work as society promised it would. What people do with that is an amazing series of movies.

Having noticed, most go on with it anyway and do what they can. The proper rejecters can accept that the world not working where they are is a mistake of some sort, and start to look for a system of new ideas that work. This can take you all over the world looking for greater values that cannot fail.

For the intellect you can't beat India, so subtle is the cultural thinking. The escape hatch of infallibility is time and karma. Endless things to do for many lives and a goal of true finality. It may be horrible now, but, later, you will be paid. It serves very nicely to allow the total poverty there to continue forever at least.

For the heart, the Middle East is the go. Poets like Rumi, Hafiz, Rabia, so beautiful. Really, they are exquisite. And the practices are beautiful. But pretty arrows on a sign is all they are. The infallibility factor is a greater quest and the moral loving high ground to stand on.

This doesn't regard the spontaneous loving kindness sometimes called 'heart' or 'love' that arises from awakening, which has no need to pursue, but regards the urgent ache of the subtle mind.

That heart and the mind are both false masters.

Pick the one that seems prettier, and easier for you to live with. Have a life. But both are not a final endless silence, nothing is sure to awaken you in either. The how to live right question is truly false. Once the person involved vanishes, life happens, it is right as it is happening. Nothing else is possible.

As gardeners go, this one is a great gardener. Astrology, on the other hand, looks like an entertainment to me. The ideology of any newly made small culture of knowing, pleasing as it might be, is exactly the same as the one it got rejected for. Another prison made of the same bricks. "Look at the new boss. Same as the old boss."

But it doesn't matter. Infinite is inclusive. Perfect.

# WHY TALK THEN?

*A*nd if you like, why stop too?

Herman Melville, much admired by Jed McKenna, wrote an extraordinary short story called 'Bartleby the Scrivener'. Bartleby lives his truth in a way that slices the world all round him away beautifully.

The experience of waking is just that. An experience. Not a deductive conclusion. It seems some situations provoke it, and some not. This must be dependent on your own particular Gordian knot. Provocative situations are individual and logically not predictable. But it seems likely that mind is self-stoking and self-preserving, so will automatically reside in safety – and avoid that which could destroy it.

Before waking all is kept in best order possible, mind and language collude gently with the physiology to construct a reality that protects them from the harm an inconsistency could do. Stability is paramount (but impossible) as reality is benign and this collusion, *ipso facto*, must exist only to avoid the discomfort of dissonance.

Reality itself has no dissonance, so a mind exists, covering the absurdity of its own manifestation, by avoiding, distorting and amplifying different bits of reality. All the automatic mechanisms sitting stored in physiology.

An awakening is a devastating blow to this collusion, a complete notification that all is a dolls' house at afternoon teatime. Baselessness is exposed instantly on all fronts. The mind simply stops, language ceases, and the body falls silent.

Endless. Freedom and gasping relief. Existence is all

round in its utter acceptance, all has come home. As though you have parked and switched off the car. Whew.

The empty remains will need to do things in the world, however. So, the car is started and moves into the world, cutting its wood and carrying its water. Although it knows stopping now, strangely the bits of it badly worn from collusion to hide are still badly worn. It still drives how it always did, but it knows how silence works. "Not this, it makes that happen; body doesn't care for that." And preferences exist.

Automatic and without motive. As they interface with the world, and its colluders... All kinds of possibilities are imagined by the minds around... He is doing this, therefore it must be because... and so on and on circling the wagons.

The old body habits are easily followed, and some are fine. Some hurt the physiology. So why do that? Don't. Prefer not to. In this, a body healing happens, but in the apparent passing of time and all gently presided over by silent loving existence.

Awake behaviour is thus not predictable. Sad for the seeking mind, but as it can't awaken anyway it can only reject and sort in a panic, to look earnestly for the nothing, deduced somewhere, in a peace-seeking, but not destroying itself, absolute frenzy.

Ideas of non-duality suit this purpose beautifully. Simple and circular, as is any functional zealotry. Absolute in its inclusion and in its exclusion.

Nothing useful can be said in terms of reality there. No pointer is possible, no science of arrival, an infinite chasm exists between the seeings. It is too vast to yell across, and for what? Seeing real is silently beautiful, all is in, no outside experience is possible. All knots and catharsis are included, but...

Some of it rattles around in the thing that sees. Old things, integrating as one goes along, all well and fine, come to visit. Questions, or a statement that isn't helpful. A choosing can happen, and in a moment one can turn an old corner and arrive in a familiar limited place. Familiar but different, with no power to uproot reality now. Still there's a flavour or a hint of the old response – the mind arrives to help with that old habit of wanting to teach or share, or just have some like unminded company.

A ghost town. In choosing to speak yet again ... "No I looks like this ..." And the ghost town fills with the clatter of earnest seeking argument in less than a microsecond. And then... Leave?... Or stay? Body feels icky. However, what awareness *loves* more than anything is to see itself awake. The thrill of finding an empty, in a body. Omigod! So it talks.

So, staying, engaging, rattling the can, it all happens, ever so hopefully..

Until the body has taken enough, then it's time to rest.

That's all. No opinion, no judgement, nothing. Rest. Tea. Garden. Birds and leaves, no mediator needed, just loving silent reality. Ah, home again...

"Oh, what a day I have had beloved..."

As to talking, argumenting, pointing, smacking this, liking that... I suddenly am tired and right there with Bartleby.

"I would prefer not to."

# I AM AN ALCOHOLIC

*T*hat's tough on the body. And it will eventually reduce the integration possible with mind too, really, for that reason alone it might be nicer for you to try and do something.

As to awake, it is so clear that nothing is excluded. Nothing. Even the feeling of undeserving that might come from behaviour the world doesn't sanction. It is without judgement and not separate from you whatever is happening..

Most of us seem to have what looks like an addictive tendency, a habit of thought and behavior that is supported by its own private Idaho in the mind and reflected into the body with complete accuracy.

It is sort of evident that it truly isn't detrimental to awakening in that it is true that awakening happens to alcoholics and has done so around us. Sailor Bob Adamson (a joy in the world that one) will tell you of his past and complete commitment to alcohol above all else for a long time. But for real insight, as Bob wasn't a drinker at the time he left the building, the person to look towards is Byron Katie. She woke up in the aftermath of a bender of monumental proportions. And it is with her still. They are the experts there.

# DRUGS

*I know this place you are talking about. I take Eccy and DMT when I can get it, it's nice to hear it talked about, but I see no reason to do anything but go on as I am, what do you think?*

Well, I don't think anything really. I remember all this, it isn't untrue, and it isn't true either. If you want to have a recreational time and see the things you carry inside, no problem.

But it is difficult in some ways for me to say nothing.

After awakening there is a deep relaxing in the body, silence and gentleness... Not much in the way of flashing lights or revelation really, more relief and surprise if anything. All the reasons from the world that held relaxation away are still there in the body. And when awake the focus is not on their machinations, more all round, having a look. When the world comes back in the area where the body has a reaction, it happens as it always does, right there in the body. Here is the moment of a sort of choice. Body watch will happen, and the real will return. Or it won't, and the world and your cultural gifts will prevail. The gentle choice to 'not take delivery' as Sailor Bob says is the relaxing one. The world goes on, the body assimilates and you act on the real, rather than the gift from other times.

As an aside, a strange third habit can come into play here, a denial, based on the thought that 'awake' has a certain form. The idea that, when awake, the world must manifest as only pleasantness, bliss and kindness. It isn't right, and the preconception will end up maintaining the collusion of the body and mind, the continuous integration of the physiology and consciousness will simply be avoided. 'Bypassing' is the current name for this.

All is welcome in consciousness. All and everything.

With drug use the process is reversed, the physiology is changed and the view of the world changes accordingly. Temporarily. In itself an experience of something apparently greater.

But.

The body takes a smacking. And if the drug is made by amateurs, then who knows what extras are there? If not, then there is doubt that the entire effect is known. This is a subtle science, if it is science at all, and twisting the physiology to shape conscious perception in this way looks brutal and unnecessary. It costs the body, and then after, there is recovery and attempts at integration on a massive scale. The perception of what is real can become suddenly a long and non-integrated distance from where it was yesterday. All so that a twisted-out physiology can produce the fantastic ideas the unconscious holds away. Including whatever you think the beyond might be.

Now it seems possible that, under certain conditions and 'expert' supervision, the experience can loosen cultural ties, adjust decently and be a useful trigger toward reality. But I see no such experts. A small number of talented amateurs and a lot of collateral damage.

I have had bliss and silence from chemical interference, and it is not the same. It isn't real in the sense that awake is. A momentary gift from the subtle mind. And the wrapping is crap.

I look at the young man, clear and delicate, thin too. It is clear that something different is happening, but delicate it certainly is. This fineness will not integrate in the world I feel. I find the truth of this later, when, while talking with him, it comes to light that he lives with the like-minded a long way from people.

I have nothing for him that he wants, we like each other, and as I left I misquoted Ram Dass to him.

*"In retrospect, LSD and the stronger psychedelics aren't really critical to the process. What they can do is show you a possibility. But once you know the possibility, to keep revisiting the possibility again and again isn't necessarily the transformative process. The process is finally to live in the world and keep transforming within the world."*

# IRRELEVANT ADVICE

"*I* am going to visit my old girlfriend tomorrow, all the old trips are up and I hate it. I thought this stuff would go away..." This is a different sort of question than I am used to. Andrew is awake, has been for awhile. He has ideas about how it should behave and, after the initial totality, as the world came back and his body demanded food and water, laundry came, his focus went there as it needed. He felt totality gone, that he was no longer awake, or at least that it was flickering.

Aaargh, it is always awkward. Now he had a hard time in relationship with this woman, no fun at the end at all. He had been hurt bad and his body remembers. So he is thinking to catch a bus to spend four days with her and is frightened and sick inside. You know how it works, it is from the perception and the naming brings the story and the body responds. It feels brand new and real. He hates it. And that is the problem right there. He hates it. And he thinks it shouldn't happen.

I can't believe it really, it is your own body with its real knowings and responses. Awake. Where is it all gonna go just because you are awake? It is in there and your own personal gift from the world. These responses are not your enemy any more than the bliss. They are all experiences, now and here. The condiments on the other hand are not. We add them. He is frightened and so be it. The rest is a story.

The fear is an old friend we have that comes when the body is reminded by circumstance; it simply is a notice that we got hurt here, be careful. It is a dear friend, an old one coming to take care of you. Why, with such a visitor, would you do other than make it welcome and be grateful for the reminder? Adding resentment and hate and any other thinking is just treating your guest badly.

And it throws focus into the mind very nicely if you take delivery of the whole package. He has the choice now, it is no longer automatic, it is another ghost town you no longer need to live in, familiar as it is. Such moments are gifts of care, and really, to be welcomed in. Given total satsang and gratefulness for the light they bring.

Look at the place, here and now, and see if the reminder is necessary, choose to act in some way. For him, simple, go visit and see, or just don't. Same with the idea that totality is gone. Give it your total loving attention. It is impossible to make a mistake. Ideas are not a final reality. They are hitchhiking and will leave as you move to another moment. Don't let them drive. Or do. Pay attention. That's all.

# NON-DUALITY PRESS

If you enjoyed this book, you might be interested in these related titles published by Non-Duality Press:

*The Light That I Am*, J.C.Amberchele
*Awake in the Heartland*, Joan Tollifson
*Painting the Sidewalk with Water*, Joan Tollifson
*Only That*, Kalyani Lawry
*The Wonder of Being*, Jeff Foster
*An Extraordinary Absence*, Jeff Foster
*Awakening to the Dream*, Leo Hartong
*Dismantling the Fantasy*, Darryl Bailey
*Standing as Awareness*, Greg Goode
*The Transparency of Things*, Rupert Spira
*Ordinary Freedom*, Jon Bernie
*I Hope You Die Soon*, Richard Sylvester
*The Book of No One*, Richard Sylvester
*Be Who You Are*, Jean Klein
*Who Am I?*, Jean Klein
*I Am*, Jean Klein
*The Book of Listening*, Jean Klein
*Spiritual Discourses of Shri Atmananda* (3 vols.)
*Nobody Home*, Jan Kersschot
*This is Always Enough*, John Astin
*Oneness*, John Greven
*What's Wrong with Right Now?*, Sailor Bob Adamson
*Presence-Awareness*, Sailor Bob Adamson
*You Are No Thing*, Randall Friend
*Already Awake*, Nathan Gill
*Being: The Bottom Line*, Nathan Gill

For a complete list of books, CDs and DVDs, please visit:
## www.non-dualitypress.com

Forthcoming books from NON-DUALITY PRESS
2011

THE ALMIGHTY MACKEREL AND HIS HOLY BOOTSTRAPS
*by* J.C.Amberchele
The headless perspective

THE ULTIMATE TWIST *by* Suzanne Foxton
A novella: addiction, love, therapy and awakening

GONER *by* Louis Brawley
The last five years with UG Krishnamurti

ESSENCE REVISITED *by* Darryl Bailey
Slipping past the shadows of illusion

THE LOVING AWARENESS IN WHICH ALL ARISES
*by* Rick Linchitz
Dialogues on awakening

BLESSED DISILLUSIONMENT *by* Morgan Caraway
Seeing Through Ideas of Self

THE LAST HUSTLE *by* Kenny Johnson
Finding true happiness and freedom in prison

THE PLEASANTRIES OF KRISHNAMURPHY
*by* Gabriel Rosenstock
Revelations from an Irish ashram

DRINK TEA, EAT CAKE *by* Richard Sylvester
Dialogues and observations of a tour in Germany

# CONSCIOUS.TV

CONSCIOUS.TV is a TV channel which broadcasts on the Internet at www.conscious.tv. It also has programmes shown on several satellite and cable channels. The channel aims to stimulate debate, question, enquire, inform, enlighten, encourage and inspire people in the areas of Consciousness, Healing, Non-Duality and Psychology.

There are over 200 interviews to watch including several with communicators on Non-Duality including Jeff Foster, Steve Ford, Suzanne Foxton, Gangaji, Greg Goode, Scott Kiloby, Richard Lang, Francis Lucille, Roger Linden, Wayne Liquorman, Jac O'Keefe, Mooji, Catherine Noyce, Tony Parsons, Halina Pytlasinska, Genpo Roshi, Satyananda, Richard Sylvester, Rupert Spira, Florian Schlosser, Mandi Solk, James Swartz, and Pamela Wilson. Some of these interviewees also have books available from Non-Duality Press.

Do check out the channel as we are interested in your feedback and any ideas you may have for future programmes. Email us at info@conscious.tv with your ideas or if you would like to be on our email newsletter list.

## WWW.CONSCIOUS.TV

### CONSCIOUS.TV and NON-DUALITY PRESS
present two unique DVD releases

### CONVERSATIONS ON NON-DUALITY – VOLUME 1
Tony Parsons – *The Open Secret* • Rupert Spira –
*The Transparency of Things – Parts 1 & 2* • Richard Lang –
*Seeing Who You Really Are*

### CONVERSATIONS ON NON-DUALITY – VOLUME 2
Jeff Foster – *Life Without a Centre* • Richard Sylvester –
*I Hope You Die Soon* • Roger Linden – *The Elusive Obvious*

Available to order from: www.non-dualitypress.com

Lightning Source UK Ltd.
Milton Keynes UK
UKOW050802291111

182881UK00001B/182/P